HODDER GCSE HISTORY FOR EDEXCEL

ANGLO-SAXON AND NORMAN ENGLAND
c.1060–88

Ian Dawson • Esther Arnott • Libby Merritt

LEARN MORE

The Publishers would like to thank the following for permission to reproduce copyright material.

Photo credits
page 2 © World History Archive/Alamy Stock Photo; **page 4** © The Granger Collection/TopFoto; **page 7** © World History Archive/Alamy Stock Photo; **page 13** © British Library Board/TopFoto; **page 19** © CM Dixon/Print Collector/Getty Images; **page 20** © Frank J.Parson; **page 21** Jewellery, 'The West Yorkshire Hoard' (gold), Anglo-Saxon/© Leeds Museums and Galleries (Leeds Art Gallery) U.K./Bridgeman Images; **page 23** *left* Here Count Guy of Ponthieu seizes Earl Harold (1022–66) detail from the Bayeux Tapestry, before 1082 (wool embroidery on linen), French School, (11th century)/© Musée de la Tapisserie, Bayeux, France/Bridgeman Images, *right* © World History Archive/Alamy Stock Photo; **page 27** © The Art Archive/Alamy Stock Photo; **page 29** © World History Archive/TopFoto; **page 31** © World History Archive/Alamy Stock Photo; **page 37** York Archaeological Trust; **page 39** *left* © Oronoz/Album/akg-images, *right* © ImagesEurope/Alamy Stock Photo; **pages 40–1** Looking over the heads of the English towards the Norman ranks during the Battle of Hastings (w/c on paper), Dunn, Peter (20th century)/Private Collection/© Historic England/Bridgeman Images; **page 42** Duke William Exhorts his Troops to Prepare Themselves Wisely Like Men for the Battle Against the English Army, detail from the Bayeux Tapestry, before 1082 (wool embroidery on linen), French School, (11th century)/© Musée de la Tapisserie, Bayeux, France/With special authorisation of the city of Bayeux/Bridgeman Images; **page 43** *top* © World History Archive/Alamy Stock Photo, *bottom* The Normans' feigned flight pursued by the English during the Battle of Hastings (w/c on paper), Dunn, Peter (20th century)/Private Collection/© Historic England/Bridgeman Images; **page 44** © GL Archive/Alamy Stock Photo; **page 54** They construct the fortifications, detail from the Bayeux Tapestry, before 1082 (wool embroidery on linen), French School, (11th century)/Musée de la Tapisserie, Bayeux, France/Bridgeman Images; **page 57** © Sussex Archaeological Society; **page 66** © Roger-Viollet/TopFoto; **page 68** © York Museum Trust; **page 71** ©Fedor Selivanov/123RF.com; **page 83** © World History Archive/Alamy Stock Photo; **page 84** © DeAgostini/Getty Images; **page 92** © The National Archives; **page 93** © The National Archives; **pages 96–7** *Norman England: 1066–1204*, by Trevor Rowley, © Osprey Publishing, part of Bloomsbury Publishing Plc; **page 99** *left* © DeAgostini/Getty Images, *right* Bishop Odo Holding a Baton Urges on the Young Soldiers, from The Bayeux Tapestry (wool embroidery on linen), French School, (11th century)/© Musée de la Tapisserie, Bayeux, France/With special authorisation of the city of Bayeux/Bridgeman Images; **page 103** © Clearview/Alamy Stock Photo; **page 110** © Mark Jones/Alamy Stock Photo; **page 112** © Ian Dawson; **page 113** © Brian Jannsen/Alamy Stock Photo.

page 66 © History Today; **page 111** The History Press, 2004.

Every effort has been made to trace all copyright holders, but if any have been inadvertently overlooked, the Publishers will be pleased to make the necessary arrangements at the first opportunity.

Although every effort has been made to ensure that website addresses are correct at time of going to press, Hodder Education cannot be held responsible for the content of any website mentioned in this book. It is sometimes possible to find a relocated web page by typing in the address of the home page for a website in the URL window of your browser.

Note: The wording and sentence structure of some written sources have been adapted and simplified to make them accessible to all pupils while faithfully preserving the sense of the original.

Hachette UK's policy is to use papers that are natural, renewable and recyclable products and made from wood grown in sustainable forests. The logging and manufacturing processes are expected to conform to the environmental regulations of the country of origin.

Orders: please contact Bookpoint Ltd, 130 Park Drive, Milton Park, Abingdon, Oxon OX14 4SE. Telephone: +44 (0)1235 827720. Fax: +44 (0)1235 400454. Email: education@bookpoint.co.uk Lines are open from 9 a.m. to 5 p.m., Monday to Saturday, with a 24-hour message answering service. You can also order through our website: www.hoddereducation.co.uk

ISBN: 978 1 4718 6175 8

© Ian Dawson, Esther Arnott, Libby Merritt 2016

First published in 2016 by
Hodder Education,
An Hachette UK Company
Carmelite House
50 Victoria Embankment
London EC4Y 0DZ

www.hoddereducation.co.uk

Impression number   10 9 8 7 6 5 4 3 2 1

Year   2020 2019 2018 2017 2016

All rights reserved. Apart from any use permitted under UK copyright law, no part of this publication may be reproduced or transmitted in any form or by any means, electronic or mechanical, including photocopying and recording, or held within any information storage and retrieval system, without permission in writing from the publisher or under licence from the Copyright Licensing Agency Limited. Further details of such licences (for reprographic reproduction) may be obtained from the Copyright Licensing Agency Limited, Saffron House, 6–10 Kirby Street, London EC1N 8TS.

Cover photos *left* © Detail Heritage/Alamy; *right* © Mary Evans Picture Library 2015

Illustrations by DC Graphic Design Ltd, Barking Dog, Oxford Designers and Illustrators and Peter Lubach

Typeset in ITC Legacy Serif Std Book 10/12pt by DC Graphic Design Ltd

Printed in Italy

A catalogue record for this title is available from the British Library.

CONTENTS

1 Introducing the Norman Conquest

On the evening of 14 October 1066 William of Normandy stood on the battlefield of Hastings. He must have been exhausted, relieved and uncertain about what would happen next. He had won the battle, but one victory did not give him control of the whole of England. Over the next few years the English rebelled time and again, but William always proved successful. William dominates this book so the best place is with William himself when he set sail to conquer England. He was nearly 40 years old. What qualities and experience did he have to help him conquer England?

1.1 William of Normandy

◀ William as shown in the **Bayeux Tapestry**. Despite William's fame we know very little about what he looked like. No one at the time wrote a detailed description of his appearance. None of the illustrations of William, such as this one from the Bayeux Tapestry or those on coins, look lifelike. They were created to show William as a powerful ruler, not to be realistic. He may have been about five feet and ten inches tall but that depends upon whether a thigh bone in his tomb is really his! The rest of the skeleton disappeared when his grave was ransacked in 1562 and we cannot be certain the thigh bone was William's. It is likely that he was very strong, as **chroniclers** suggest he could fire arrows from a heavy bow while on horseback, steering the horse with his legs. They also tell us that he had a harsh, rough voice, which probably added to his commanding appearance.

WILLIAM'S EXPERIENCE BEFORE 1066

1 Draw your own version of the table below which shows the qualities William needed to conquer and remain in control of England.

Qualities needed to conquer and control England	Evidence that William had developed these qualities before 1066
1 Military skills	
2 Keep the kingdom peaceful and secure	
3 Ability to organise a system of government	
4 Ability to win the support of his nobles	
5 Ability to raise money when needed	
6 Maintain a good relationship with the Church	
7 Produce an heir to inherit the kingdom	

2 Read the text on William's life before 1066 on page 3. Identify the qualities William possessed and add evidence of them to column 2 of your table.

3 Draw the continuum line below. Using your completed table, decide where to place each of the qualities on the line.

| −2 | −1 | 0 | +1 | +2 |

William's experiences and qualities most likely to lead to failure   **William's experiences and qualities most likely to lead to success**

4 Which of William's qualities do you think were most valuable for:
   a) winning the Battle of Hastings and defeating rebellions?
   b) establishing long-term control over England?

NORMANDY

Normandy means 'land of men from the north', because the area was taken over by Vikings. One of the Viking leaders, Rollo (William's great-great-great grandfather), created the **Duchy** of Normandy in the 900s. By the time William became Duke in 1035, the people of Normandy were culturally French. This means that they spoke the French language and followed the Christian religion. Normandy also had close links with the country of France but was an independent state. Duke William enjoyed absolute power over his land.

Nowadays the country of France contains Normandy, but in the eleventh century France was a much smaller kingdom and Normandy, Anjou and Flanders and others were independent states.

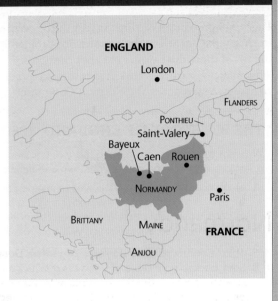

This page focusses on William to introduce the theme that acts as the spine of the book. However, you are about to learn a great deal about England and its people on the next few pages and Chapter 2.

William's life before 1066

William was born about 1027, the son of Robert, Duke of Normandy, and Herleva, the daughter of an undertaker and tanner. His parents were not married, which is why he is sometimes referred to as 'William the Bastard'. William became Duke of Normandy before he was eight after his father's death in 1035. Violence then erupted between Norman lords and knights who fought over land and power, putting the young Duke in danger. On occasion he was hidden in poor people's cottages to keep him safe. William finally won complete control of Normandy in 1047 when his army defeated his cousin's who was trying to take over Normandy.

Controlling Normandy

William stamped out opposition ruthlessly. When the town of Alençon rebelled against him, he chopped off the hands and feet of 32 of its inhabitants. However, William also won support by giving important positions to local landowners. They realised there were benefits in supporting William – if they didn't, he would take their land away and exile them. William also won the support of religious leaders who were very influential. He appointed Odo, his half-brother, as Bishop of Bayeux, one of the most powerful positions in the Norman Church. William was deeply religious, attending Mass most mornings, and he built spectacular cathedrals and monasteries in Normandy.

Building Normandy's power

William's first objective as duke was to make Normandy more secure. He was especially concerned about the threat from the Count of Anjou, whose lands lay to the south of Normandy. In 1049, he led his army to defeat Anjou and in the 1050s he twice defeated invasions by the combined forces of Anjou and France. On one occasion, he attacked as his enemies were crossing a river, making it hard for them to deploy their forces effectively. William proved himself a brilliant strategist, especially skilled in building and capturing castles. William ensured that other rulers in northern France supported Normandy by conquering Maine and defeating Brittany. By 1060, William was secure from attacks by other rulers and dominated northern France. He could not have considered invading England if Normandy had still been threatened.

Marriage and heirs

William married Matilda, daughter of the Count of Flanders, a powerful landowner in northern France. The marriage therefore added to William's power and influence. William and Matilda had nine children, four of them boys.

Visible learning

Improving your vocabulary

One of the keys to success in history is communicating clearly and precisely. We return to this on page 9 but, as a starter, make sure you understand the highlighted words and phrases and also identify any other words you do not understand. This will get you ready to tackle the Word Wall on page 9.

1.2 The Big Story of England, 1060–88

Pages 4–5 provide an outline history of the events you are studying. Starting with this outline – the Big Story – helps solve one problem some students have. They know the details of individual events but they cannot 'see' the whole story of the Norman Conquest. This makes it harder to link events together to explain their causes and consequences and to assess the impact of the Norman Conquest.

THE BIG STORY OF ENGLAND, 1060–88

We want you to dive into the Big Story of England, 1060–88, and then retell it yourself. These questions will help you create your own outline account.

1 a) Why did people risk their lives to invade England?
   b) Why did William have the opportunity to become England's king?
   c) Was it inevitable that William would win the crown? Give two reasons for your answer.
   d) Identify three ways in which William's rule changed life in England.

2 Was William's conquest completed in a) 1066 b) 1071 c) 1075 d) 1087? Justify your answer.

3 Look back to your table of William's qualities on page 2. What other evidence of his qualities can you identify on this page?

4 **This is the core activity on this page!** You have up to two minutes to tell the outline story of the Norman Conquest. Work in a group of three to plan and tell your story. Use each of these words or phrases:

   opportunity   turning point   consequences   rivals   succession crisis

5 a) After you have told your story – write it down! This is important to help it stick in your brain. Think about how to make it memorable by using headings, colours and illustrations to identify key moments.
   b) Describe or draw one illustration to go with each section of your story.

Check you know the meaning of the **highlighted** words.

The King and his country in 1060

England was ruled by Edward the Confessor who had been king since 1042. England was a wealthy country. There was a flourishing system of trade in towns and overseas and the **Anglo-Saxons** were excellent farmers, trading the produce and animals they farmed. The King's most powerful supporters were the **earls**, who owned huge areas of land. The most powerful were two brothers from the Godwin family, Harold and Tostig Godwinson.

The Godwin brothers become rivals

Tostig was Earl of Northumbria, but in 1065 his people rebelled against him because of his cruelty. Some of the rebels marched south to discuss their issues with Edward, who asked Tostig's older brother, Harold, Earl of Wessex, to meet them. After the meeting Harold advised Edward to listen to the rebels and remove Tostig to avoid **civil war**. Tostig fled abroad angry that his brother had opposed him. Now the brothers were enemies, but Harold was even closer to the king.

◀ A silver coin, one of many in circulation during King Edward's reign, used for trade. It is stamped with a picture of Edward in profile.

The succession crisis

Edward and his wife, Edith, had no children. A succession crisis was looming and there seemed to be at least four possible successors. Two were Englishmen – Harold of Wessex, the most powerful man in England, and fourteen-year-old Edgar Aethling, Edward's great-nephew. There was also William, Duke of Normandy, and, to add to the crisis, Tostig was encouraging Harald Hardrada, King of Norway, to vie for the crown.

The battles of 1066

At the end of 1065, King Edward fell into a coma. He died on 5 January 1066. Next day the Witan (the powerful lords and bishops who were the king's advisers) agreed Harold of Wessex should be king and he was crowned immediately. When this news reached William he made plans to invade as did Harald Hardrada. In September, King Harold's problems arrived all at once. The Norwegian army landed and, at the Battle of Fulford, defeated Edwin and Morcar, Harold's loyal earls in the north. Therefore, King Harold, who had been guarding the south coast, had to march his army north to stop Hardrada over-running the north. King Harold did beat the Norwegians at the Battle of Stamford Bridge, but as soon as he had done that he heard that William had landed in the south. After another rushed march, Harold was defeated and killed at the Battle of Hastings.

Taking control of England

On Christmas Day 1066, William was crowned King, but he only really controlled the south-east corner, a small part of England. He certainly feared rebellions and tried to avoid pushing the English into rebellion. He allowed many Englishmen to keep their lands and the leaders of the Church to remain as bishops.

However, rebellions did break out and between 1067 and 1071 William seemed constantly on the march, dealing with rebels. In 1069 his hold on England seemed to waver when there was a large rebellion in the north, supported by a Danish invasion. William put down the rebellion with great brutality and gave the lands of Anglo-Saxon landowners to his nobles and knights. Even then, rebellions were not over as another broke out – unsuccessfully – in 1075.

A different England?

William built castles throughout England as protective bases for his soldiers and all the cathedrals were rebuilt on a much larger, dominating scale. William needed a strong Norman government because he spent most of his time in Normandy after 1072, putting down rebellions there and defending Normandy from attacks by neighbouring lords. In England, new laws punished attacks on Normans and higher taxes were collected. Normans replaced Englishmen as bishops. Government and church services were conducted in Latin, which was incomprehensible to many Anglo-Saxons, though gradually Norman-French words were added to people's everyday language. In 1085 William's power was demonstrated when he ordered the great Domesday Survey, identifying who held each piece of land in the country and how much it was worth. Even so, historians still argue that there was much from Anglo-Saxon society that continued despite William's rule. In many ways, William built on ideas and government methods already in existence.

William's death

William died in 1087 while on campaign against a French enemy. His second son, William Rufus, was crowned King of England, but was briefly challenged by rebellious nobles who wanted Rufus's older brother, Robert, as king. The Normans had clearly conquered England as it was now Normans, not Englishmen, fighting each other for the crown.

▲ This is a simple outline. It is not the complete story. You will learn many more important details later in the book.

1.3 Introducing the key characters

WHO WERE THE KEY CHARACTERS?

Below you can see the main people you'll meet in this book. Some of their names will be familiar from pages 2–5.

1 Draw your own large copy of this chart and add biographical details to each person – use the Big Story, your own knowledge and research to help you. Include each person's main role in the events of 1060–88.

2 Add lines to your chart showing family links such as brothers or parents and children.

3 Asking questions about the past is an important historical skill to develop. Make a list of at least **five** questions you want to ask about the people on this page. These question starters may help.

What …?	To what extent …?
Who …?	What happened …?
Why …?	How significant …?
How …?	What effects …?
When …?	

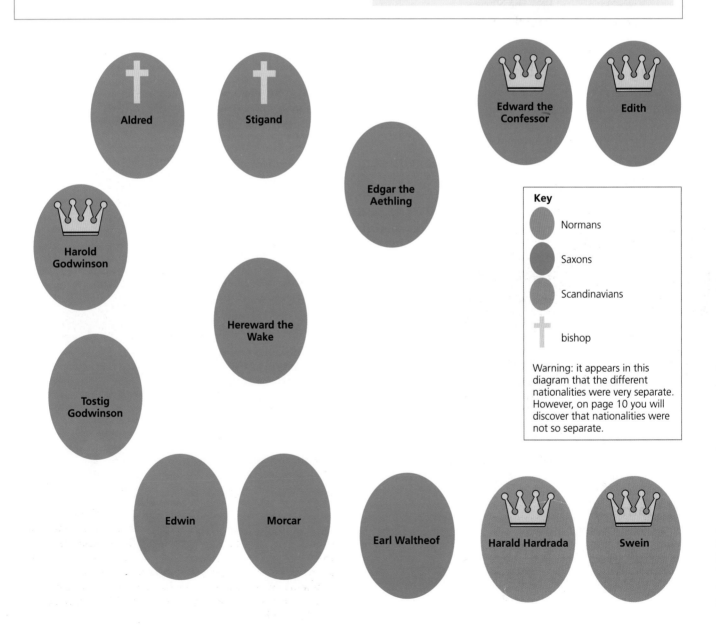

Aldred

Stigand

Edward the Confessor

Edith

Harold Godwinson

Edgar the Aethling

Tostig Godwinson

Hereward the Wake

Edwin

Morcar

Earl Waltheof

Harald Hardrada

Swein

Key

Normans

Saxons

Scandinavians

✝ bishop

Warning: it appears in this diagram that the different nationalities were very separate. However, on page 10 you will discover that nationalities were not so separate.

Visible learning

Remembering the people

Some students find it hard to remember the names of all the people in this topic, especially as we do not have pictures or descriptions of them to stand out in our memories. However, it is important for your exam that you know who all the people were and what they did.

Therefore, the chart and activities help you start on what may be a difficult task. You won't remember all the individuals straightaway, but if you keep returning to the chart you'll be surprised how soon you do know 'who's who'.

You could do this activity physically in the classroom with each of you 'playing' one of the characters and telling the others who you are, which others you are connected to and what your role was in the Norman Conquest. And, if you're brave enough, explain what you thought of William!

William

Matilda

Odo

Lanfranc

Robert of Normandy

William Rufus

Henry

▲ William I

Earl Roger

Earl Ralf

Visible learning

Why we are making learning visible?

Studying history isn't always straightforward. When you meet new information it's easy to feel puzzled, even totally confused! When you feel puzzled it is vital to identify exactly what you don't know or understand. These 'visible learning' boxes will help you by identifying common problems that students have – make misunderstandings visible – so you can identify your own problems and then put them right.

1.4 Was William really almost six feet tall?

You read about William's appearance on page 2. The exact words were:

He may have been about five feet and ten inches tall but that depends ...

The key words above are '**may have been**' and '**that depends ...**' . They reveal that we are not certain about William's height because there is not enough good evidence to allow is to be certain.

William's height is a helpful example of an important issue when we study this period of history:

We are often uncertain about the answers to questions about the Norman Conquest.

The activity below provides an example of the problems of using sources for this period to explore one of many important questions.

THINKING ABOUT THE SOURCES

You can see below details of six sources that provide evidence about the Norman Conquest.

1 Imagine you are trying to answer the question:

How fairly did William treat the English after he became King in 1066?

Where would you place each source on the continuum line below?

1	2	3	4
Unlikely to be at all helpful for answering the question	May provide a little evidence but overall is likely to be misleading or inaccurate	May provide some useful evidence but may also be misleading or inaccurate	Likely to be very helpful for answering the question

2 Explain your placing of **two** of the sources.
3 Why do you think it is difficult to provide certain answers about some aspects of the Norman Conquest?
4 Identify two questions about the Norman Conquest that you think could be answered with some certainty using one or more of these sources.

A The Bayeux Tapestry was embroidered in the 1070s. Historians believe that William's half-brother, Odo, asked for the Tapestry to be made. It was embroidered by nuns in England. It shows the events leading up to William's invasion and then the Battle of Hastings.

B William of Jumieges was a monk who lived at the abbey of Jumieges in Normandy. He wrote a history of the Dukes of Normandy in 1070. William may have spoken to men who were at Hastings, including William the Conqueror who visited Jumieges in 1067.

C Orderic Vitalis was born near Shrewsbury in England in 1075. He had an English mother and Norman father and was sent to live in Normandy when he was a boy. He became a monk in Normandy and wrote his history around 1125. His account of the events of the 1060s was partly based on the histories written by William of Jumieges and William of Poitiers but his account from 1071 is his own work.

D William of Poitiers was a Norman priest. At one time he was Duke William's personal priest and regarded him as a hero. In the 1070s he wrote a history called: *The Deeds of William, Duke of the Normans and King of the English.*

E The Anglo-Saxon Chronicle was a year-by-year record of events that had been kept since the 870s. There were different versions, each slightly different, written by monks in several monasteries. In 1066 two monasteries were still keeping their chronicle up to date.

F John of Worcester was an English monk who lived in the monastery at Worcester. He wrote a history of England about 70 years after 1066. The early parts of John's chronicle are the same as the Anglo-Saxon Chronicle, but John wrote his own account of the Norman Conquest. He took his information from other English accounts that had been written earlier.

1.5 Concluding the Introduction!

Part 1: Language is power!

chronicler   consequences   tanner   probably   Duchy

earls   nobles   possibly   bishops   Flanders

strategist   absolute power   Witan   succession crisis   kingship

turning points   Latin   trade   may have been

We mentioned the Word Wall on page 3 so here it is – or the beginning of it. While you work on this topic, create your own Word Wall, maybe on a large piece of A3 paper. Add new words after each key topic in the book. Building your own Word Wall helps you to:

- understand the meaning of technical words and phrases that relate to life in the eleventh century
- communicate clearly and precisely when you describe or explain historical events; this definitely helps you do well in your exams
- spell these important words correctly.

You will give yourself the best chance of doing well in your exams if you take responsibility for your own learning. You need to identify words:

- whose meaning you are not sure of
- you can't spell correctly every time

and make sure you find out their meaning.

BUILDING YOUR WORD WALL ?

1 Copy the wall above but use different colours to highlight:
   a) technical words and phrases that relate to life in the eleventh century
   b) words that help you communicate precisely when you explain the causes or consequences of events.
2 Add to your wall at least two more words from this chapter that you expect to be useful when writing about the Norman Conquest.

PART 2: HOW SHOULD WE REMEMBER WILLIAM THE CONQUEROR? ?

Later in this book we will return to William himself and sum up the evidence that helps us answer the question above. A good way to keep track of the evidence is to create a diagram like the one below.

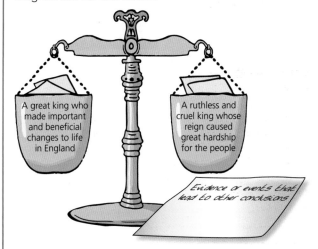

A great king who made important and beneficial changes to life in England

A ruthless and cruel king whose reign caused great hardship for the people

Evidence or events that lead to other conclusions

Think back over Chapter 1. Which events would you place on the set of scales or on the sheet alongside it?

KEY TOPIC 1

Anglo-Saxon society and the Norman Conquest, 1060–66

This key topic contains three chapters which tell the story of the first stage of the Norman Conquest. Here are the questions you will be exploring:

1 How should we describe Anglo-Saxon society?
2 Why was there rivalry for the throne in 1066?
3 Was William's leadership the main reason for the Norman victory at the Battle of Hastings?

Visible learning

Separating the detail from the 'big picture'

You do not need to remember events before 1060 for your exam. What you need to remember is the 'big picture' of the links between the countries and of the nationalities of the kings.

ENGLAND – A SEPARATE COUNTRY? **?**

1 Identify the information on this page that shows statements A and B are wrong.

2 Rewrite A and B to give an accurate picture of the links between countries.

3 Which information suggests that other countries might become involved in events in England when King Edward died in 1066?

England – a separate country?

First, however, this page explores two misunderstandings which make it harder for students to make sense of what happened in 1066. Here are those misunderstandings:

A
England and Normandy were entirely separate countries which had little contact.

B
It was very unusual for England to be ruled by a foreign king.

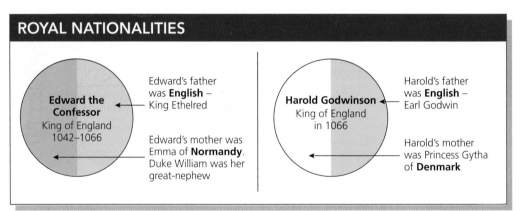

ROYAL NATIONALITIES

Edward the Confessor
King of England
1042–1066

Edward's father was **English** – King Ethelred

Edward's mother was Emma of **Normandy**. Duke William was her great-nephew

Harold Godwinson
King of England in 1066

Harold's father was **English** – Earl Godwin

Harold's mother was Princess Gytha of **Denmark**

1002	1015	1016	1017	1035	1040	1042
King Ethelred II of England married Emma, the sister of the Duke of Normandy.	Vikings, led by King Swein of Denmark and his son Cnut, invade England. Emma sent her son Edward to Normandy to keep him safe.	King Ethelred of England and his son, Edmund Ironside, died. Cnut of Denmark became King of England. He was married to an English noblewoman called Aelgifu and they had a son known as Harold Hare-foot.	King Cnut married Emma (the widow of King Ethelred) although Aelgifu remained Cnut's lover. Cnut and Emma had a son called Harthacnut.	King Cnut died. He was succeeded by his son Harold who was half-English, half-Danish.	King Harold Hare-foot died. He was succeeded by Harthacnut who was half-Danish, half-Norman.	King Harthacnut died. He had no children, so his , half-brother Edward (the Confessor) was crowned King of England. Edward was the son of King Ethelred (English) and Emma (Norman).

2 Anglo-Saxon society

What pictures do you have in your mind about Anglo-Saxon England? You may have seen the beautiful jewellery discovered at Sutton Hoo. This treasure suggests the Anglo-Saxons had very sophisticated skills. You might have been to the rebuilt Anglo-Saxon village at West Stow, where the homes may look simple and primitive.

'Sophisticated' and 'primitive' are good descriptive words but they are generalisations – words that make very general statements about a period or people. In this chapter you will look at Anglo-Saxon society more closely and decide how best to describe a variety of aspects of English life. These aspects cannot have been both 'sophisticated' and 'primitive'. So what are the best words to describe each aspect of society in the chart below?

DESCRIBING ANGLO-SAXON ENGLAND

1 Draw a copy of the table below. Allow plenty of space to add words and phrases in the topic boxes.

2 Choose two or three words from the Word Wall below to describe each topic and pencil them into your table. Use pencil because you may wish to change them later. Don't be tempted to look ahead in the chapter yet; we want you to base your answers on what you think you know now.

3 Read pages 12–20. After reading about each topic, decide if you want to change any of your original words and make a final choice of five words for each topic.

4 Choose evidence to support your choice of words. For example, if you chose 'small' to describe villages, what evidence from pages 16–17 shows this word is accurate?

Social system		Monarchy and central government		Local government and the earls		Legal system	
Description	Evidence	Description	Evidence	Description	Evidence	Description	Evidence

Village life		Town life		The economy		The Church	
Description	Evidence	Description	Evidence	Description	Evidence	Description	Evidence

backward   superstitious   agricultural   lawless   well-organised   complex

primitive   poverty-stricken   ignorant   simple   crude   violent

low-technology   efficient   disorganised   small   large   advanced

sophisticated   centralised   hard   religious   hierarchical   war-like   wealthy

diverse   powerful   localised   listened to advice   delegated   law-abiding

2.1 The social system

Anglo-Saxon society was hierarchical, which means it was arranged in a clear order of rank or status. Everyone knew their status, and what was expected of them. This page sets out the social ranks, the work people in each rank did, and their responsibilities.

A person's status could increase if they paid for it. A slave could save up and buy his freedom to become a peasant. A ceorl could become a thegn if he built up a large estate. People could move down in status if they committed a crime. Anglo-Saxon law ruled that some crimes were punishable by being made a slave.

▲ The king's most important tasks were to defend his country from attack, to pass good laws and to make sure the laws were obeyed. He also had power over the Church.

▲ The earls were the most powerful lords and owned huge areas of land. There were usually no more than six earls. They were the king's advisers, ensured the king's laws were enforced in their regions, and raised men for the king's army. They were expected to protect people on their lands from attack.

▲ Thegns (less than one per cent of the population) were nobles, but less powerful than earls. They were primarily warriors who defended the king. In return he granted them land. They carried out local duties such as guarding tax collectors from attack and organising the repair of fortifications, roads and bridges.

▲ Ceorls (roughly ten per cent of the population), sometimes called freemen, owned their own small area of farmland. Being free meant they did not have to work for their lord every week, unlike the peasants and slaves. All male ceorls had to serve in an army if needed.

▲ Peasants (over 70 per cent of the population) had to work on the lands of their lord for up to three days a week and do any job he requested, such as taking animals to market. On other days they farmed their own rented land to grow enough food to survive and pay their rent (which could be paid in money or goods, like pigs, eggs or milk). Every male peasant could be asked by their lord to fight in wartime.

◄ Slaves (around ten per cent of the population) were not free and had no land. They worked on their lord's land or in his house as servants. Their master dictated every aspect of their life, including the amount they worked, the food they ate, and sometimes even who they should marry.

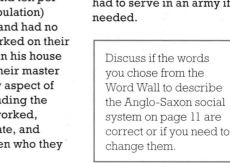

Discuss if the words you chose from the Word Wall to describe the Anglo-Saxon social system on page 11 are correct or if you need to change them.

2.2 Monarchy and central government

The king was the head of the government and took all the important decisions. His most important tasks were to:

- defend his country and his people from attack, usually by commanding the army himself; military skills were therefore important, although not essential
- pass good laws and to make sure the laws were obeyed
- defend the Church and appoint its leaders
- manage his earls and other nobles so they co-operated with his decisions and helped him run the country effectively. The king was the only person with the power to settle disputes between the nobles. The best kings used a combination of two things to manage their nobles – they rewarded nobles with land and wealth and dominated them with their strong personalities.

Today there is a large civil service to do all the administration governments need. In the eleventh century, kings had only a small number of administrators. The administrators wrote down the king's laws and sent out written orders called writs to officials around the country.

The groups of people helping the king were known as the royal household and the royal court. The diagram explains who these groups were. The household and court were not physical buildings but groups of people who moved around the country with the king.

The king's household consisted of the king, his family and his household soldiers, called housecarls, plus the servants needed to care for the royal family.

The king

The court consisted of the king's household plus his advisers – the chief landowners and bishops who the king consulted on important decisions.

The Witan

When kings needed advice on important issues they called a meeting known as the Witanagemot, or Witan – an Anglo-Saxon word meaning 'meeting of wise men'. The Witan did not have regular meetings or a regular membership. It met whenever the king decided to hold a meeting and only those he summoned could attend. The men summoned included earls, thegns and senior members of the Church, including archbishops and bishops. Even then the king took the final decisions. However, by consulting the most powerful men in the country, he had shown that he respected their views and they were more likely to support his decisions.

The Witan's most powerful role came if there was doubt about who would be the next king. Then the Witan could meet and make a recommendation or decision, but in most cases the real decision was made by whoever had the most military support. We will return in more detail to the question of how the crown was inherited on page 28.

Discuss if the words you chose from the Word Wall to describe monarchy and central government on page 11 are correct, or if they need changing.

◀ An eleventh-century illustration of an Anglo-Saxon Witan. The king sits in the middle, wearing his crown and holding a sceptre and sword to symbolise his authority. In the background a man is being hanged to symbolise the power of the king over the lives of his people and his responsibility to ensure laws were kept.

2.3 Local government and the earls

The king was the centre of government, so he and his administrators are known as 'central government'. However, the king could not govern every part of the country directly from the centre. He needed other people to govern each local area, making sure criminals were punished and taxes were collected. This work and the officials who did it are described as local government.

The very top layer of local government consisted of the earls, the most powerful landowners. The four main earldoms were Wessex, Mercia, Northumbria and East Anglia (see map). In these vast areas the earl was expected to ensure that there were no rebellions and that crimes were punished and armies were raised for the king. Earls were therefore second only in power to the king and could rival the king if they banded together.

However, earls owned such large areas that they were not able to collect every tax or punish every crime in their lands. Therefore, kings had created a more detailed system of local government that was very effective – the shires and the hundreds.

The shires and the hundreds

There were about 40 shires or counties. The king appointed a local thegn as sheriff (shire-reeve) – his chief official in each shire. The king sent him instructions in documents called 'writs'. Sheriffs were expected to:

- collect taxes and fines due to the king
- carry out justice in the king's shire-court; shire-courts dealt with the most serious crimes – murder, theft and disputes over the ownership of land
- raise soldiers for the royal army whenever they were needed.

The hundreds (called wapentakes in the north) were sub-divisions of shires. Hundreds each contained around twelve villages. Each hundred had its own **reeve** who held a hundred-court each month to deal with less serious crimes.

2.4 The legal system

The shire- and hundred-courts were the heart of the legal system, along with the king's laws. These laws were very detailed, although kings had to accept that there were different legal customs around the country. In parts of Northumbria, for example, men still took part in the blood-feud. If a relative was killed or injured, family members believed they had the right to take their own revenge, often through violence, rather than taking the criminal to court for punishment. Blood-feuds, however, often led to more violence, so kings preferred other punishments which reduced the chance of further violence and crime.

Punishments

1 **Wergild** – this was a fine paid to the victims of crime or their families as compensation. The level of fine was laid down in the king's laws and is a reminder of the hierarchy of Anglo-Saxon England. The wergild for killing a nobleman was 300 shillings, for killing a freeman was 100 shillings and for killing a peasant was even lower.

There were also fines for injuring different body parts. The wergild for a disabled shoulder was 30 shillings, a severed thumb 20 shillings and a lost big toe 10 shillings. This was probably because most Anglo-Saxon men were farmers or craftsmen so thumbs and shoulders were important. Without them a man's ability to farm his land and earn money for his family was far less.

▲ The major Anglo-Saxon earldoms in 1065.

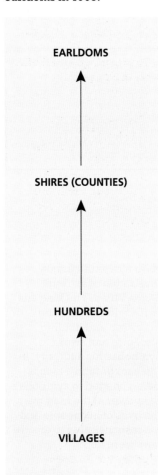

EARLDOMS

SHIRES (COUNTIES)

HUNDREDS

VILLAGES

2 **Capital punishment and physical punishment** – a small number of serious crimes carried the death penalty, such as **treason** against the king or betraying your lord. This was to deter others and show the importance of loyalty to the king. As the Church was exceptionally important, anyone who stole from churches paid a fine and suffered the extra punishment of having a hand cut off.

Reoffenders were also punished harshly. Punishment for repeat offenders included mutilation, such as cutting off a hand, ear or nose or 'putting out' the eyes. Prisons were rarely used because they were expensive to build and run as gaolers would have to be paid and prisoners fed. Therefore, prisons were only used for holding criminals before trial so they could not escape.

Policing

Anglo-Saxon England did not have police forces. People lived in small communities so they could keep an eye on each other's behaviour. Therefore Anglo-Saxon kings created a self-help system known as a tithing. Every male over the age of twelve joined a tithing, a group of ten men who were responsible for each other's behaviour. If one broke the law, the other members of the tithing had to bring him to court, or pay a fine. This meant there was collective responsibility for stopping crime.

If a crime was committed the victim or witness was expected to raise the 'hue and cry'. The entire village was expected to down tools and join the hunt to catch the criminal. If a person did not join the 'hue and cry' then the whole village would pay a hefty fine.

Trials

The Anglo-Saxons used two types of trial:

1 Trial by jury in the hundred- or shire-court. The jury consisted of men who knew both the accuser and the accused. The accuser and accused gave their version of events and it was up to the jury to decide who was telling the truth. If there was no clear evidence the jury made their decision based on their knowledge of the people concerned.

2 When the jury of a hundred- or shire-court could not decide on a person's guilt, the accused was subjected to trial by ordeal in a church. This shows the importance of religion, because it was God who became the judge in trials by ordeal. Before the ordeal the accused had to fast for three days and hear Mass. There were different kinds of ordeal. Trial by hot water, for example, involved the accused plunging his hand into boiling water to pick up an object and lift it out. If the resulting wound healed cleanly, it was a sign from God that the accused was innocent. If it did not heal, they were guilty and should be punished.

▲ The members of a tithing were of all ages.

> Discuss if the words you chose from the Word Wall to describe the Anglo-Saxon government and legal system on page 11 are correct or if they need changing.

◀ Trial by hot water to prove whether this man was innocent or guilty.

2.5 Village life

The church was one of the most important buildings in the village. Many churches were built of wood, although by the eleventh century some were being rebuilt in stone.

An earl's personal estate included a large wooden hall for entertaining and feasting. Inside was a bare earth floor, but the walls were decorated with tapestries and the earl's gold and valuable items would be on display. Some had their own private chamber for sleeping.

Ploughs were among the most valuable items in a village as they were essential for making the fields ready to grow crops. A team of eight oxen was used to pull a plough.

Not all villages had an earl's personal estate within them. Those villages far from an earl's estate would be subject to visits and checks from the earl or his men.

There were many millions of sheep, which were used for their wool, meat and milk. Pigs, cows, chickens and geese were also reared, which required plenty of land for pasture (fields for feeding animals).

A house was one large room with a fire in the centre (so the smoke could escape from a small hole in the roof) and different zones for cooking, sleeping and sitting. Animals would be brought in when the weather was particularly bad because peasants and ceorls relied on them for work and food and didn't want to run the risk of them dying in the cold.

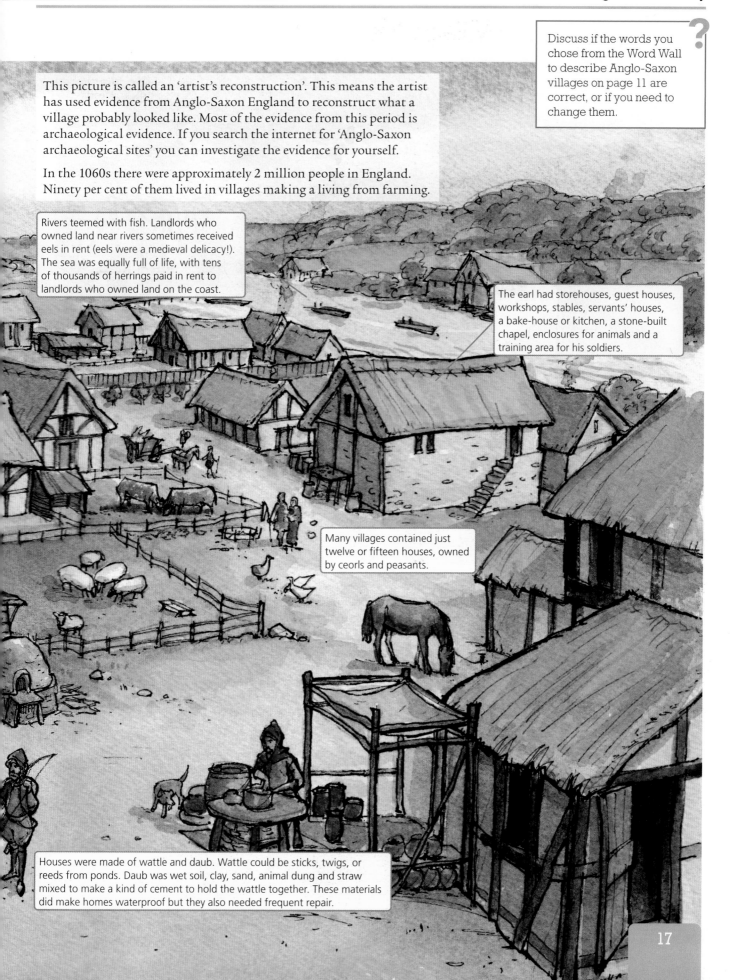

Discuss if the words you chose from the Word Wall to describe Anglo-Saxon villages on page 11 are correct, or if you need to change them.

This picture is called an 'artist's reconstruction'. This means the artist has used evidence from Anglo-Saxon England to reconstruct what a village probably looked like. Most of the evidence from this period is archaeological evidence. If you search the internet for 'Anglo-Saxon archaeological sites' you can investigate the evidence for yourself.

In the 1060s there were approximately 2 million people in England. Ninety per cent of them lived in villages making a living from farming.

Rivers teemed with fish. Landlords who owned land near rivers sometimes received eels in rent (eels were a medieval delicacy!). The sea was equally full of life, with tens of thousands of herrings paid in rent to landlords who owned land on the coast.

The earl had storehouses, guest houses, workshops, stables, servants' houses, a bake-house or kitchen, a stone-built chapel, enclosures for animals and a training area for his soldiers.

Many villages contained just twelve or fifteen houses, owned by ceorls and peasants.

Houses were made of wattle and daub. Wattle could be sticks, twigs, or reeds from ponds. Daub was wet soil, clay, sand, animal dung and straw mixed to make a kind of cement to hold the wattle together. These materials did make homes waterproof but they also needed frequent repair.

2.6 Town life

Ten per cent of people in Anglo-Saxon England lived in towns. A town was a place that had a defensive wall, a mint (where coins were made) and a marketplace. Some were located on the sites where Roman towns had been and they incorporated Roman features such as the stone fortification walls.

In many ways, as you can see above, towns looked very like villages. Houses were built from the same materials as houses in a village – wattle and daub. They were usually built on narrow plots, often near to a river for water supplies. However, many people living in towns had higher status and more money than people in the countryside, even if their houses were much the same.

Another similarity with villages was that there were animals inside towns and grazing in fields outside the walls. Crops were also grown in fields outside the town by townspeople. This farming provided food for the townspeople and they could also sell their produce on market day.

By 1060 around a hundred places were described as towns, but compared with today Anglo-Saxon towns were extremely small. London (called Ludenwic) was the largest, with around 10,000 people. It was a great trading town but was not the capital city. The next largest group of towns had up to 5,000 people. They included York (Eoforwic), Southampton (Hamwic) and Winchester. Winchester was more like the capital city as it was the place where most of the king's treasure and important documents (such as laws) were kept.

The markets in towns sold a wide range of goods that were not made in villages. These included jewellery, leather items such as bags, woven cloth and weapons. Some traders also sold luxury goods like wine from France, pepper from Asia or the East Indies, fine cloth (like silk), spices and gems from Spain, Italy and the Middle East.

> Discuss if the words you chose from the Word Wall to describe Anglo-Saxon towns on page 11 are correct, or if you need to change them.

2.7 The economy

The village economy

Villages had an agricultural economy. Peasants and ceorls were chiefly farmers, using their plots of land to grow crops of wheat, barley and vegetables, and to raise animals. However, many developed craft-skills and made goods such as pottery, iron weapons, tools and woven cloth. They produced just enough food and clothing, pots and other goods for their own family – this is called a subsistence economy.

Some people produced a little extra to barter (or swap for other things). This is called an exchange economy. Many more goods were sold by bartering than in exchange for coins. A peasant could barter milk, for example, in return for pottery bowls. He could also take his produce to the weekly market in a local town to sell in exchange for money, which he might then save to buy a new animal.

> **The economy**
> How people earned their living (e.g. what kinds of farming and trading took place) and how wealthy the country was.

The urban economy

In towns the economy was predominantly an exchange economy. Towns held weekly markets where people would bring goods to sell. Craftspeople could sell their goods alongside traders who visited the town for the market day. Some of the craftspeople came from nearby villages, but a town such as York contained specialist leather workers, silversmiths and textile workers, and many had shops and workrooms in the town.

Towns on the coast or on large rivers were important ports for international trading routes. England **exported** its wool, iron and cheese; we even have records of slaves being traded to Ireland from Bristol. England **imported** precious metals, glass, wine, gems and spices which were then sold at markets.

Although a lot of goods were exchanged by barter on market day, Anglo-Saxons also bought and sold using coins. All coins were silver pennies and most of the silver for the coins came from Germany, which highlights the links Anglo-Saxon England had with other countries. Once the silver was imported, the law said that coins could only be made in towns (in the mint) so production had to be overseen by a royal official.

▲ A silver penny from Harold's reign, showing the king's face. Historians estimate that 9 million silver coins were in use in 1066. Pennies were valuable coins. A sheep cost 5 silver pennies, a pig 10 silver pennies and an ox cost 30 silver pennies. Although peasants did use coins to make larger purchases from the market, such as an animal, it was the earls and wealthy members of society who depended on coins to buy, for example, military equipment or the luxury goods that showed their status.

> 1 What is the meaning of these words and phrases?
>   a) subsistence economy   d) mint
>   b) barter   e) exchange economy
>   c) market
>
> 2 Discuss if the words you chose from the Word Wall to describe the Anglo-Saxon economy on page 11 are correct, or if you need to change them.

ARCHBISHOPS

↑

BISHOPS

↑

PRIESTS

2.8 The influence of the Church

The Anglo-Saxon Church influenced life in England in two ways:

1 It was very rich and powerful and played an important part in the government of the country.
2 It played a big part in everyday life in all villages and towns.

The Church, power and government

The Church was very clearly organised. At the top were the two archbishops, of Canterbury in the south and York in the north. Each archbishop was in charge of the Church in his region. There were also about fifteen bishops, each one in charge of an area called a diocese or see. The bishops were responsible for making sure the village priests obeyed the Church's laws and carried out religious services properly.

There were also many abbeys – monasteries and convents, which housed monks and nuns respectively. They were headed by abbots (monasteries) and abbesses (nunneries). The main task of the monks and nuns was to pray, but they also wrote histories, created beautiful tapestries and acted as teachers and advisers to lords. Selling crops grown on monastery farms also made the monasteries wealthy. The Church was therefore a very powerful and rich organisation. It owned 25 per cent of the land in England. Its archbishops and bishops were often members of the Witan and acted as royal advisers.

▲ Most churches and cathedrals were rebuilt after the Norman Conquest and during the period from 1100–1500, but some Anglo-Saxon churches remain. This is the tower of the church in Earls Barton which was built in the late tenth century.

The Church and everyday life

Anglo-Saxons believed that Heaven and Hell were real places. They knew that after death their souls would go to Heaven or Hell, depending on how religious they had been and how well they had lived. Therefore it was vital for their souls that people went to church to worship God. This meant that the priest in each village had a very important role, safeguarding the people and their souls.

People also prayed regularly because they knew that God played a major part in their everyday lives. They believed that God sent diseases or healed the sick and sent good harvests or bad harvests which decided whether they had enough to eat through the winter and spring. Religion also played a big part in celebrations and holidays. People did not work on the major **Holy Days** of the religious year – Christmas, Easter and others – and they celebrated **saints' days**, often with feasting and games. This meant that they had plenty of opportunity for time away from work in the fields.

Visible learning

Church and churches

The word 'church' has two meanings. Church with a large C is the organisation which is in charge of religion.

In contrast, church with a small c is the building in which religious services are held.

Using 'Church' and 'church' in the right ways shows you understand the difference and the topic.

Discuss if the words you chose from the Word Wall to describe the Anglo-Saxon Church on page 11 are correct, or if you need to change them.

2.9 Conclusion: Describing Anglo-Saxon England

▲ You can view this hoard, and many others, online. Try a web search for 'Anglo-Saxon hoard'.

This picture shows the West Yorkshire hoard, discovered in 2008 by a metal detectorist. The items date from the seventh to the eleventh centuries. The ring with the red jewel (a garnet) was perhaps owned by a bishop or earl. The gold content of the ring is very high. This is just one of many finds that reveal the amazing wealth of Anglo-Saxon England.

DESCRIBING ANGLO-SAXON ENGLAND ?

Now that you have completed your work on this chapter, look at your table from page 11 and make sure you have now chosen the words that best describe each topic and you have identified evidence to support your choice of words.

1 Now choose five words or phrases that you think best sum up Anglo-Saxon England.

2 Identify two things that have surprised you or are most memorable about Anglo-Saxon England and explain your choices.

3 Create a Word Wall of your own that includes all the words and phrases about Anglo-Saxon society that you might need to use in your exam.

Visible learning: Revise and remember

Later in this book we shall include regular activities to start you on the path to effective revision. You need plenty of knowledge to do well in your exams and you need to work at making that knowledge stick in your brain. The more you recap what you have learned and identify what you are not sure about, the more chance you have of success. This single activity begins your 'Revise and remember' activities. Answer the questions below, identify what you don't know, and go back and find the correct answers.

Test yourself

1 Name three of the chief earldoms.
2 What was the king's chief official in each county called?
3 What was the Anglo-Saxon word for 'wise men'?
4 What name was given to the rank of nobles below the earls?
5 What was a tithing?
6 List two major responsibilities of Anglo-Saxon kings.
7 What name is given to free villagers?
8 Name two of the largest towns in England.
9 What was a mint?
10 Name two items imported from overseas.
11 What were hundreds?
12 Where did trial by ordeal take place?
13 Describe two features of:
   a) the Witan
   b) the Anglo-Saxon legal system
   c) village life
   d) the work of the king.

3 1066: Death, succession and claims to the throne

3.1 The house of Godwin

In 1065 the Godwins were by far the most powerful family in England. The family tree below shows you the members of the family, but behind those names lie some remarkable and dramatic stories. Even the family's origins are obscure. Godwin was probably the son of a rebel and pirate in the south of England – a very wealthy rebel and pirate who owned a lot of land!

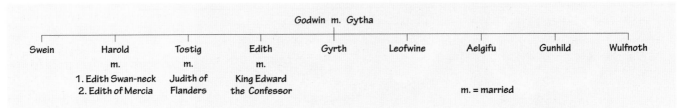

Godwin m. Gytha

Swein	Harold	Tostig	Edith	Gyrth	Leofwine	Aelgifu	Gunhild	Wulfnoth
m.	m.	m.					
1. Edith Swan-neck	Judith of	King Edward				m. = married	
2. Edith of Mercia	Flanders	the Confessor					

▲ The Godwin family tree. Swein should have been Godwin's heir as Earl of Wessex, but he abducted a nun and fled abroad, then murdered his cousin and finally died when walking barefoot to Jerusalem to show his sorrow for his actions. The sons of Earl Godwin are known as, for example, Harold Godwinson to identify their family clearly.

Earl Godwin himself married Gytha, the daughter of a Danish earl, which won him many Danish allies. Godwin was at the centre of government in England under both King Cnut and then Edward the Confessor. He supported Edward when he became king in 1042 and his daughter, Edith, then married King Edward. When Godwin died in 1053 he was succeeded by his son, Harold, as Earl of Wessex, the richest earldom in England. Together with his brothers, Harold continued to build up the family's power and wealth. The clearest evidence of this is the fact that in 1065 the Godwinson brothers were significantly wealthier than King Edward himself. Edward's lands produced an income of around £6,000 a year but the Godwinsons received around £8,500 a year from their lands.

> ### ACTIVITY ?
> This is a complex family story. Could you create a visual version, a diagram or a flowchart to help you recall the important events and people over the next three pages?

Harold Godwinson, Earl of Wessex

Despite his power and the fact that he became king, we do not know a great deal about Harold. We do not even know for certain what he looked like. We do know that one of his major achievements was to put an end to widespread violence and rebellion in Wales on behalf of King Edward. Between 1055 and 1063 he and his brother, Tostig, led a series of military campaigns in Wales to end the violence caused by rebellious local princes.

Harold's wealth and military success won him many supporters. Many local thegns gave him their support and in return they were well rewarded by Harold for their loyalty. Harold also developed strong links to some of the most influential bishops, winning the support of the Church. He certainly showed evidence of a strong religious belief, founding the abbey at Waltham in Essex and going on pilgrimage to Rome.

Harold also won allies in the east of England because he made an unofficial marriage (known as a 'Danish marriage') with a rich landowner in the region, Edith Swan-neck. Such 'marriages' were common but are described as 'unofficial' because they did not take place in a church. This marriage lasted at least twenty years and Harold and Edith had at least five children. However, at the beginning of 1066, Harold made an official marriage with another Edith, the sister of Morcar, Earl of Northumbria, and Edwin, Earl of Mercia. This marriage may well have taken place to win the support of Morcar and Edwin for Harold's kingship.

Harold's embassy to Normandy

The best-known and most intriguing event in Harold's life before 1066 was his embassy to Normandy around 1064. The story of this visit is told in the Norman sources written after 1066 in great detail. Nearly half the space in the Bayeux Tapestry is devoted to Harold's visit. As they tell it, it's a really good, dramatic story! Here's a modern summary of the Norman version of events:

> Around 1064 King Edward sent Harold to Normandy as his ambassador to confirm the King's promise of the crown to William. Harold's ship was blown off course and he landed in the territory of Count Guy of Ponthieu, who held Harold prisoner. When William heard this news he made sure Harold was freed – which put Harold in William's debt. Harold then joined William's army when William was fighting local enemies and, on one occasion, Harold even saved some of William's men from drowning – in the Tapestry Harold is shown pulling a man out of quicksand. William and Harold therefore worked together successfully, and as a reward William is shown in the Tapestry giving Harold a full set of chain-mail armour and helmet, a great mark of respect.

> All that, however, is scene-setting for the climax of this part of the story – Harold's oath to William. According to the Norman sources Harold then took an oath – a promise made on religious relics – renewing the King's promise to William of the English throne. They also say that in addition Harold swore loyalty to William and promised to help him become king of England after Edward's death.

> The Bayeux Tapestry and other sources then leap forward to Edward's death and Harold's coronation, showing that Harold had broken that sacred oath. He therefore deserved to die at Hastings for breaking his oath to William.

That is the Norman story. It is so full of detail that it is very believable, but it only appears in sources after 1066. In contrast, most English sources do not mention Harold visiting Normandy at all! However, this is not surprising as, writing after 1066, they said little about the background to the Norman Conquest and would not have wanted to portray Harold as an oath-breaker. One English writer in the early 1100s, Eadmer, does say that Harold went to Normandy, but went on his own initiative to ask William to free two of his family who were being held as hostages there. Eadmer says Harold was then forced by William to take an oath and, even then, one of his brothers was not set free.

So did Harold go to Normandy? Probably – it's a very detailed story to make up if it did not happen at all! Nevertheless, that does not mean the story of the oath is true in every detail – the Norman sources do not even agree on where Harold took the oath – but we will never know exactly what happened. We still have to keep using those important words 'probably' and 'possibly'!

▼ The Bayeux Tapestry shows Harold being captured by Count Guy of Ponthieu.

▼ Here Harold receives the armour and weapons of a knight from William.

Harold and Tostig

Look at the map below. There is one important name missing from it. It is the name of Tostig, Harold's brother. Tostig had been made Earl of Northumbria in 1055, a very important but difficult responsibility. As earl over the whole of the north, Tostig had to raise armies to defend the north against Scottish invaders, and to defend the north-east coast against Danish and Norwegian raiders. However, Tostig was never accepted by the people of Northumbria. They seem to have been suspicious of him because he was an outsider from the south. When they challenged his authority, he dealt with them very heavy-handedly. This made him even less popular. To make matters worse, Tostig spent a lot of time away from Northumbria at King Edward's court.

In October 1065, the thegns of Yorkshire rebelled against Tostig and occupied York, killing Tostig's officials and calling for a new earl. They wanted Morcar, the brother of the Earl of Mercia, to replace Tostig. King Edward sent Harold Godwinson to speak to the rebels. Harold probably realised that Tostig could not keep control of Northumbria and this would weaken the defence of the north of England. Therefore, Harold recommended that King Edward accept the rebels' demands. Morcar became Earl of Northumbria. Tostig left England and went into exile abroad.

These events made the brothers Harold and Tostig enemies. Tostig accused Harold of encouraging the rebellion against him. He tried to raid the coast around the east of England, but Earls Edwin and Morcar defeated him. When Harold became king no one knew how Tostig would react – would he make peace with his brother or continue to cause trouble?

THE GODWIN FAMILY

1 How great was the power of the Godwin family at the beginning of 1066?

2 What do Harold's campaigns in Wales suggest about his skills?

3 Why might Harold have married early in 1066?

4 What, for the Normans, was the most important part of the story of Harold's embassy to Normandy?

5 Why are we not certain about the details of Harold's visit to Normandy?

6 Why did Tostig lose his earldom of Northumbria?

7 Why might Tostig be a danger to Harold when he became king?

8 a) Make two lists – one of reasons why Harold might be a success as king and the other of reasons why he might not be successful.
   b) 'Harold was bound to fail as king.' Do your lists support or challenge this statement? Explain your answer.

◀ This map shows the areas controlled by the earls at the time of King Edward's death in January 1066. In the south most of the land was held by Harold Godwinson and his brothers, Gyrth and Leofwine. The other major earldoms, Mercia and Northumbria, were held by the brothers, Edwin and Morcar. They were also Harold's brothers-in-law.

3.2 Thinking about the rivalry in 1066

Your enquiry for this chapter investigates why there was rivalry for the crown in 1066. Before you begin the enquiry on page 26, use the time-chart below and your existing knowledge to begin thinking about possible reasons why there was such rivalry.

1 Who were the four possible rivals for the crown?

2 What evidence in the time-chart helps to explain why there was rivalry for the crown?

3 How might evidence such as the West Yorkshire Hoard (page 21) explain why there was rivalry?

4 a) What evidence in the time-chart shows that historians are not completely certain about what happened at this time?

   b) Why do you think they are not completely certain?

1002 King Ethelred II of England married Emma, the sister of the Duke of Normandy.

1015 King Swein of Denmark and his son Cnut began a campaign to take control of England. Emma sent her son Edward to Normandy to keep him safe.

1016 King Ethelred and his son, Edmund Ironside, died. Cnut, already King of Denmark, became King of England too.

1042 Edward, the son of Ethelred II and Emma of Normandy became King of England after the deaths of Cnut and his sons.

1043 Edward married Edith, the daughter of Earl Godwin and sister of Harold Godwinson.

1051 Edward invited William, Duke of Normandy, to his court. Edward and Edith had no children and Edward allegedly promised to make William heir to the throne.

1053 Earl Godwin died. His sons inherited his lands. Harold became Earl of Wessex, the richest earldom in England.

1055 Tostig Godwinson (Harold's brother) became Earl of Northumbria, increasing the family's power.

1057 Edward needed an heir. Some sources claim that Edward convinced his nephew and possible heir, Edward the Exile, to return from Hungary. Edward the Exile died not long after returning to England. His son, Edgar, lived in Edward the Confessor's court. He was the only living blood relative of the King, but in 1066 was only aged about 14.

1064 Edward allegedly sent Harold Godwinson to Normandy to repeat Edward's promise to William. Some sources say that Harold swore an oath to support William's claim to the throne.

1065 There was a rebellion against Tostig in his earldom of Northumbria. Harold advised the King to remove Tostig from power. Harold and Tostig became enemies and Tostig went abroad, perhaps to Norway and Denmark.

1066 January Edward died. Some sources claim that just before he died he entrusted his wife and his kingdom to Harold Godwinson's 'protection'. Next day, the Witan nominated Harold Godwinson as Edward's successor and he was crowned King Harold II. When he heard the news, William of Normandy started planning to invade England.

1066 spring King Harald Hardrada of Norway prepared to invade England. He allied with Tostig, who was still very angry with Harold.

3.3 Your enquiry: Why was there rivalry for the throne in 1066?

1066 – In this year King Edward died on 5 January and was buried next day in the newly-consecrated church at Westminster. And Earl Harold succeeded to the realm of England, just as the king had granted it to him and as he had been chosen for the position. And he was consecrated king on 6 January.

That extract from the Anglo-Saxon Chronicle tells a simple story. All looks straightforward – the king has died and his successor has taken the throne. There is no sign of disagreement over who should be king. However, as you know, the reality was very different. This chapter explores why the succession was not as simple as it looks and there was so much rivalry for the throne.

Creating your hypothesis

A hypothesis is your first suggested answer to the enquiry question. Here are the reasons which could have contributed to the succession crisis:

The wealth of Anglo-Saxon England	The claim and motives of William of Normandy	English customs about the succession	The claim and motives of Harald of Norway

The nature of Harold's succession	King Edward died without a strong blood heir	King Edward's attitude to the succession

Visible learning

Knowledge Organisers

The thermometer and the table are examples of Knowledge Organisers. They help you avoid the mistake of making such detailed notes that you cannot see the main points you need. Knowledge Organisers focus on recording the key points you need. They help a lot with revision too.

1 Draw a copy of the thermometer below. Use your existing knowledge to place each reason on the thermometer. Use pencil because you may change your judgements as you work through this chapter.

Irrelevant: This reason plays no part in explaining why there was rivalry	Possible: There was a chance that rivalry would develop because of this reason	Likely: This reason made rivalry likely but not inevitable	Inevitable: Rivalry would definitely develop because of this reason

2 Look at the reasons on your thermometer. Write a paragraph summing up your hypothesis which you will develop as you work through this enquiry.

3 **a)** Use the table below to collect evidence of the effects of each reason. Begin by using your knowledge of Anglo-Saxon society to complete the top row of the table. Some evidence for the first reason has been modelled for you.

   b) Now use pages 27–31 to complete the table for the other reasons for rivalry.

Reasons	How does the reason help to explain the rivalry?	Your judgement – was this reason irrelevant or did it make rivalry possible, likely or inevitable?
The wealth of Anglo-Saxon England	England's wealth came from farming, trade in precious metals and cloth and from people's skills making jewellery, gold and silver objects. Gaining this wealth must have been a major reason for people to want to be king.	This made rivalry at least possible, maybe even likely.

3.4 Refining your understanding of the rivalry for the throne

A: English customs about the succession

Today the qualification to be the next king or queen is simple – the nearest relative of the monarch is the heir. The situation was not so straightforward in the eleventh century. There were no hard and fast rules about the succession. There had even been two occasions (in 1016 and 1035) when the throne had been seized by force. However, when there was a peaceful succession, three factors were important in making someone acceptable as king:

1 Being a blood relative of the previous king – although this did not necessarily mean that the king's *nearest* relative would be the next king.
2 Being identified as his successor by the previous king.
3 Being accepted as king by the English nobles.

It is therefore important in this enquiry that you ignore modern ideas about there being a 'rightful heir', or of the king's nearest relative being the 'legitimate' heir to the crown. Ideally, the next king would be the son or close relative of the last king, but this depended on the individuals involved (Was he an adult? Did he have plenty of support? Could he defend the country?) and on the circumstances at the time of the king's death.

THE LESSON OF KING EDMUND IRONSIDE

It is easy to think that if King Edward had had an adult son then there would not have been a succession crisis, but the events of 1016 prove this is not necessarily true. In 1016 King Ethelred's son, Edmund, inherited the crown. Edmund was called 'Ironside' because of his bravery in battle, but this did not stop the Danish King, Cnut, continuing his attempt to conquer England. Edmund fought back strongly but when he died Cnut became king of England. So even a strong warrior heir could not guarantee a trouble-free succession.

SUCCESSION CUSTOMS ?

1 Look at the text on English customs. How well qualified was Harold to be Edward the Confessor's successor?

2 What can you learn from the events of 1016 about the succession?

3 a) Complete row 2 in your table on page 26.
   b) Review where you placed this reason on your thermometer. Do you need to change its placement? Use your table on page 26 to explain your judgement.

B: Edward died without a strong blood heir

King Edward and his wife Edith did not have any children. This meant Edward did not have a direct heir who could inherit the crown. Historians cannot be completely sure why they had no children. Some historians suggest that either Edward or Edith was infertile. Others claim that Edward resented Edith's family, the Godwins, being more powerful than him and did not have sex with Edith in retaliation. Another group of historians suggest that Edward was pious (he was, after all, later known as Edward the Confessor) and so felt he must be celibate. Most historians now believe that they probably did have sex, but just did not have any children. However, we cannot know why.

▶ This scene from the Bayeux Tapestry shows Edward's death. His wife Edith is at the top, her hand to her head as if crying.

Edgar Aethling

Whatever the reason, Edward having no children was a problem. Having an adult son was the best way of ensuring the safety and security of the kingdom. An adult male heir was most likely to prevent power struggles between ambitious warriors and nobles, or invasion by an ambitious foreign leader.

However, Edward did have a male relative who could have been identified as his heir. This was his great-nephew, Edgar Aethling. Edgar was a member of the Saxon royal family because he was descended from King Ethelred (look back to the time-chart on page 25 to remind yourself about Ethelred). This family link is why Edgar was given the name 'Aethling', which means 'throneworthy' and suggests that at one time he was seen as a possible future king.

In the late 1050s King Edward may have thought about identifying Edgar as his successor, but he had changed his mind by the time he died in 1066. There are two reasons why Edward and his lords did not regard Edgar as suitable to take the throne – and why the Witan did not choose him as king after Edward the Confessor died.

1 Edgar was only about fourteen when Edward died and so would not provide strong military leadership against invasions.
2 He did not have any supporters among the earls to support him as king. The earls backed Harold instead.

WHY WAS EDWARD CALLED 'THE CONFESSOR'?

Edward was given the title 'the Confessor' when he was made a saint by the Pope in 1161. 'Confessor' was the title given to saints who died a natural death rather than being murdered because of their support for Christianity.

EDWARD'S LACK OF A STRONG BLOOD HEIR

1 Why was it important for the king to have an adult male heir?
2 Why was Edgar called the 'Aethling'?
3 Why was Edgar not identified as Edward's heir?
4 a) Complete column 2 in your table on page 26.
   b) Do you need to change the placement of this reason on your thermometer? Use your table on page 26 to explain your judgement and think about these questions:
      i) If Edward had had an adult son, would this have guaranteed no rivalry?
      ii) If Edward had identified Edgar Aethling as his heir, would this have prevented rivalry?

C: King Edward's attitude to the succession

EDWARD'S PROMISES

You will be using the table below with the text on the following page to investigate how Edward's attitude to the succession contributed to the crisis.

1 Complete the table below. Some boxes have been started for you – read them carefully, then add your own further ideas.

	Where and when did Edward's alleged promises take place?	Why might Edward want this person to be king?	Why might Edward not want this person to be king?
William, Duke of Normandy		Edward was fighting with Earl Godwin in 1051. He may have wanted William's support and protection.	Edward invited Edward the Exile to return to England after 1051. This suggests he was still unsure about who should be heir.
Harold Godwinson			

2 Why is it so difficult for historians to be sure about Edward's intentions?
3 a) Complete column 2 in your table on page 26.
   b) Now review where you placed this reason on your thermometer. Do you need to change its placement? Use your table on page 26 to explain your judgement.

It is easy to assume that Edward made one decision about the succession and kept to it. However, we have to remember that he was king for over twenty years and in that time it's quite likely that his views changed, or that events made him change his views about his successor. As a result, Edward may well have identified different successors at different times in his reign. This changing of attitudes and uncertainty contributed to the crisis and rivalry that occurred after Edward's death.

A promise to William?

Norman chroniclers wrote that Edward promised the throne to William in 1051. Edward did probably feel close to the Normans throughout his reign – his mother was Norman and he spent nearly twenty years there in exile. However, another reason may also have played a part in a promise to William. In 1051, Edward quarrelled with Earl Godwin and may have wanted to make certain that neither Godwin nor his family had a chance of taking the throne. Thus Edward may have promised the throne to William instead.

However, Edward may have changed his mind about William as his successor. Edward had a blood relative called Edward the Exile. Later in the 1050s the King invited Edward the Exile to return from Hungary to England, and historians wonder if this was to consider the Exile as his successor. Edward the Exile died in 1057, leaving his son Edgar Aethling as King Edward's nearest relative. As you have read above, King Edward may have thought about identifying Edgar as his successor but had changed his mind before he died in 1066.

The story of the promise to William is even more complicated than that, as you have read on page 23. Norman sources tell us that, around 1064, King Edward sent Harold Godwinson to Normandy to renew the king's original promise to William. They also say that Harold swore loyalty to William and promised to help him become King of England after Edward's death. If this is true, it was not recorded in English accounts. Some historians think it is unlikely that Harold would promise to help William. Unfortunately, we cannot be sure what actually happened. It is possible that Harold made the promise because he was in France and dependent on William's protection after he was captured by one of William's enemies.

A promise to Harold?

English sources tell us a very different story about the succession. One version of the Anglo-Saxon Chronicle (see page 26) says that Edward 'granted' the kingdom to Harold. A second version tells us that Edward 'the wise ruler entrusted the realm' to Harold and asked Harold to 'protect' his wife, Edith, and the kingdom.

Whether this second version of the Anglo-Saxon Chronicle means Edward was actually naming Harold as his successor is open to debate – is 'protection' the same as 'rule'? Second, this event was not a public event. Naming a successor was meant to be something done in public, so that there could be no doubt about who was chosen.

It is worth looking back to Edward's death-bed scene in the Bayeux Tapestry on page 27. Edward seems to be reaching out his hand to Harold – is he choosing Harold as his successor? If it is, then it is a remarkable picture for the Tapestry to include.

If Edward did decide to grant the crown to Harold we do not know why he did so. He may have believed that Harold would make a strong king. Perhaps he was pressured by his wife (Harold's sister) and Harold to make this decision. We simply do not know what Edward was thinking.

◀ This image from the Bayeux Tapestry shows Harold Godwinson swearing an oath of loyalty to Duke William of Normandy.

D: The nature of Harold's succession

Harold Godwinson was quickly crowned as the new King of England after Edward's death. Unfortunately, no records survive from the meetings that took place between members of the Witan, so we cannot be sure why they supported Harold. It is likely that, given his phenomenal power, wealth and military experience, he was the man most likely to rule England effectively. If the Witan feared an invasion from overseas, then Harold must have seemed to have a much better chance of defending England than did young Edgar Aethling. In practice, Harold was the only strong English candidate.

The members of the Witan may also have been influenced by the desire to keep their own lands and power. With Harold as king they would keep their lands and power, but this would not be guaranteed if there was a foreign king who would want to reward his own supporters.

However, there are some signs of hostility to Harold's succession. He was elected and anointed immediately after Edward died. This was unprecedented and suggests that Harold was in a hurry, perhaps anxious about opposition if there was delay. Some kings had waited up to a year to be crowned. An English monk called Herman, writing later in the eleventh century, said that Harold not only used speed, but that he cleverly also used force (in other words the threat of his own power and wealth) to secure the throne on the same day as King Edward's funeral. Herman thought it was very distasteful for Harold to turn Edward's funeral into his own coronation.

Herman's account is especially interesting because he worked alongside the Abbot of Bury St Edmund's, who was Edward's doctor and was probably present at the time of the King's death. It suggests that not everybody in England approved of Harold taking the throne so quickly.

Nevertheless, there was no strong opposition to stop Harold from being crowned king. Nor was there opposition to him raising two large armies to fight for him at Stamford Bridge and Hastings. This suggests that questions about the legality of Harold's succession only became important later, after he had been killed in battle. If he had beaten William at Hastings, the Norman chroniclers who said Harold had not been legally crowned would never have made those accusations.

HAROLD'S SUCCESSION ❓

1 Draw a spider diagram to summarise the reasons why the Witan supported Harold as king.

2 Why was Harold's coronation unusual? What does that suggest about the strength of his claim?

3 a) Complete column 2 in your table on page 26.
   b) Now review where you placed this reason on your thermometer. Do you need to change its placement? Use your table on page 26 to explain your judgement.

E: The claims and motives of Harald Hardrada of Norway

CLAIMS AND MOTIVES

It is important to be clear about the difference between motives and claims. Motives were the reasons why individuals wanted to be king. Their claims were their justifications for being king – their relationship to the kings of England or a promise made by King Edward. Motives could include their claim if they believed that they had a right to be king, but we do not know what was in their minds.

Harald's motives: Harald Hardrada was King of Norway. Before he became king, Harald was forced to flee from Norway when it was invaded by King Cnut of Denmark. While he was in exile, he gained a great deal of military experience. He went to Constantinople, joined an army of mercenary soldiers and fought in many places. He returned to Norway with considerable wealth and many followers. This allowed him to conquer Norway and become King. However Harald wanted to conquer even more land and gain more power. Tostig Godwinson encouraged Hardrada to invade England following his brother Harold's coronation.

Hardrada means stern or hard ruler.

Harald's claim: Hardrada had a weak claim to the English throne based on an agreement made between King Harthacnut of England and King Magnus of Norway that, if one of them died childless, the other would take his throne. Harthacnut did die childless but his throne was inherited by his half-brother, Edward the Confessor. So when Edward died childless, Harald used this past agreement to claim the throne. In practice his claim was based on the power of his battleaxe.

F: The claims and motives of William of Normandy

William's motives: William was an experienced soldier and ruler and had made successful conquests in France. His ancestors had also built up their power by conquering neighbouring lands. By becoming King of England, William would acquire more land and wealth and continue to extend the power of Normandy.

William's claim: There were three different aspects to William's claim. He argued that:

1 King Edward had promised him the throne in 1051.
2 Harold had reaffirmed this promise and pledged to help William become king; Harold had therefore broken his oath when he was crowned and deserved to lose his life.
3 Harold's coronation was unlawful because it was performed by Archbishop Stigand who the Pope had said was corrupt and should not be archbishop.

▲ This map shows the location of Norway and Normandy.

▲ This scene from the Bayeux Tapestry clearly shows Stigand standing next to Harold as if he had just placed the crown on Harold's head. In contrast, English sources say that Harold was crowned by Aldred, the Archbishop of York.

THE CLAIMS AND MOTIVES OF HARALD AND WILLIAM ❓

1 Complete this table to help you remember the claims and motives of Harald and William.

	Motives	Claim to the throne
William, Duke of Normandy		
Harald Hardrada		

2 Do you think it was the motives of these two men or their claims to the throne that drove them to invade England in 1066?
3 a) Complete column 2 in your table on page 26.
   b) Now review where you placed these reasons on your thermometer. Do you need to change its placement? Use your table on page 26 to explain your judgement.

Visible learning

Changing your mind is fine! Part of getting better at history is engaging in a process of thinking, then reflecting and revising your hypothesis as you learn more and more.

3.5 Communicating your answer

Now it's time to complete your enquiry. If this was an examination, your enquiry question would look slightly different. It would say:

Explain why there was rivalry for the throne in 1066.

Now it's time to write your answer and ... **STOP!** Before you begin writing you *must*:

Revise your hypothesis and get your summary answer clear in your mind.

This is vital, because one of the biggest mistakes that students make is starting to write their answer without having the answer clear in their minds.

1 Return to your thermometer diagram and table from page 26. Use your completed notes to make sure you are certain about where each reason goes on the thermometer.

2 Use the completed thermometer to write a paragraph summarising your answer to the question.

Now it's time to write your answer!

This chapter has given you a good deal of help, and you will find more guidance in the Writing Guide on pages 114–123. However, the person who will give you the best advice is your teacher, because he or she knows exactly what help you need to improve your work in history.

And remember your Word Wall!

Here are some words that will help you write accurately and with confidence. What else can you add from this chapter?

embassy   blood relative   customs   Aethling   elected   anointed

oath   celibate   Confessor   exile   infertile

incited   trigger   this bred ...   this compelled ...   encouraged

root of   drove   origins   brought about   fundamental   allowed

this meant that ...   this led to ...   this resulted in ...

Visible learning

'This meant that ...' – using connectives to tie in what you know to the question

WHAT YOU KNOW   WHAT THE QUESTION ASKS

When talking or writing about a reason, you cannot just say that it led to rivalry. You have to **prove** that it led to rivalry. You can do this effectively by using some of the golden words and phrases in the Word Wall such as 'this meant that ...', 'this led to' and 'this resulted in ...'.

We call these words and phrases **connectives** because they connect what you know to the question and prove they are strongly linked.

Practice questions

Use the guidance on pages 114–123 to help you write effective answers to these questions.

1 Describe two features of:
   a) the power of the Godwin family
   b) William of Normandy's claim to the English throne
   c) Harold Godwinson's embassy to Normandy.

2 Explain why Earl Harold of Wessex became king of England in 1066.

3 'The main reason why there was rivalry over the throne in 1066 was because Edward the Confessor did not have a son.' How far do you agree? Explain your answer.

Some of your exam questions (such as questions 2 and 3 above) will suggest two topics you could use in your answer. You can see examples on pages 118–121.

We have not included topics in the practice questions in this book to give teachers the opportunity to change the topics with questions from year to year.

Remember that questions as well as topics change every year.

3.5 Visible learning: Developing independence

On page 7 we introduced the idea of making learning **visible** – if you can see and describe how you go about learning, you will learn more effectively. This page is a crucial example of 'visible learning'. What you see below is your route-map – how to get from knowing a **little** about a topic to knowing a **lot** about it. It is important because in the future you will need the skills to study independently, perhaps at A level, university or at work. The route-map or process below will help you work independently and effectively. The box below shows the process in six stages. Then the diagram explains it more fully.

Questions ⟹ Hypothesis ⟹ Research ⟹ Answer ⟹ Communicate ⟹ Revise

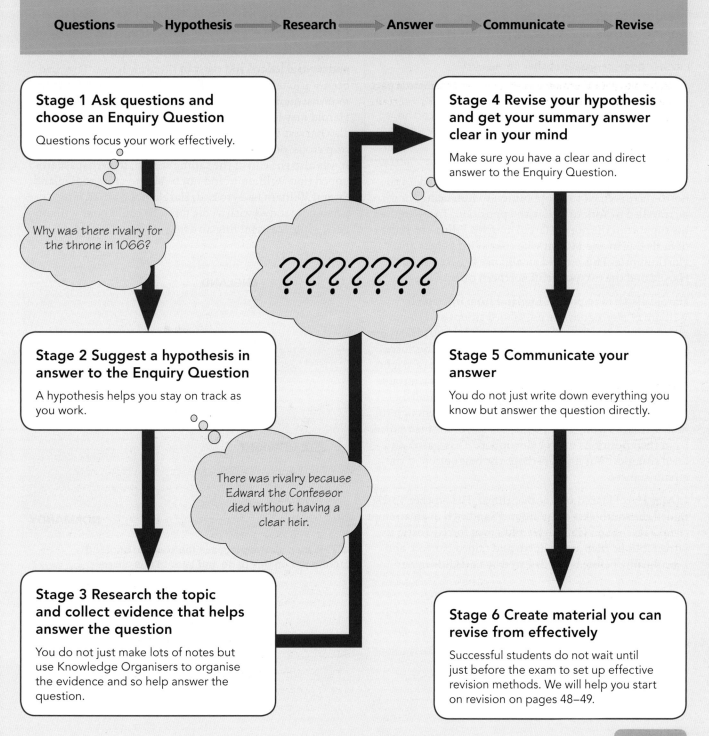

Stage 1 Ask questions and choose an Enquiry Question

Questions focus your work effectively.

Why was there rivalry for the throne in 1066?

Stage 2 Suggest a hypothesis in answer to the Enquiry Question

A hypothesis helps you stay on track as you work.

There was rivalry because Edward the Confessor died without having a clear heir.

Stage 3 Research the topic and collect evidence that helps answer the question

You do not just make lots of notes but use Knowledge Organisers to organise the evidence and so help answer the question.

Stage 4 Revise your hypothesis and get your summary answer clear in your mind

Make sure you have a clear and direct answer to the Enquiry Question.

Stage 5 Communicate your answer

You do not just write down everything you know but answer the question directly.

Stage 6 Create material you can revise from effectively

Successful students do not wait until just before the exam to set up effective revision methods. We will help you start on revision on pages 48–49.

4   1066: Invasions and battles

4.1 Preparing to face invaders

EARLY THREATS TO HAROLD ?

Read the information on this page and answer these questions.

1   How did Harold try to secure the loyalty of the north?

2   Tostig did not successfully invade England, so why did his actions create problems for Harold?

3   a)   Why did Harold send many of his troops home in September 1066?

   b)   How would you describe his decision to send his troops home – foolish, necessary, a calculated risk or in some other way?

Harold's worries began soon after he was crowned. In the north there seemed to be opposition to him being King, so he travelled to York to deal with opposition. To strengthen his support in the north Harold married Edith, the sister of Earls Edwin and Morcar who controlled Mercia and Northumbria. This created an alliance between King Harold and the two powerful northern earls.

Harold also had to protect England from invasion by William of Normandy. He positioned troops and ships along the south coast to keep watch, but had no idea where William would land, so he was forced to spread his forces out. Harold himself took up position on the Isle of Wight – sailing from there would have given Harold a favourable wind to swoop down on William, wherever he landed. Harold hoped that even a small force would be enough to hold William's troops back while the rest of his men sailed from their positions to provide support. This wasn't an ideal situation, but it was perhaps the best option in the circumstances.

In May Harold faced yet another threat. His brother Tostig raided the south-east coast around Sandwich in an attempt to take revenge on Harold. Harold's men forced Tostig to retreat, but he then sailed north and raided Norfolk and Lincolnshire before being defeated by Earls Edwin and

Morcar. Tostig then fled to Scotland. It is at this point that historians think Tostig made contact with King Harald Hardrada of Norway, convincing him it was a good time to invade England and promising his support for Hardrada.

By September, Harold's troops were becoming restless and he decided to send most of the army home. They had been stationed on the south coast keeping watch for many months: many had become bored and were underfed. Harold may have worried about losing their loyalty. It was also harvest time and men were needed in their villages to reap crops, or next spring their families would go hungry. It was also the end of the sailing season, so perhaps Harold hoped that William would not be able to cross to England. Even if William had crossed, Harold hoped that, if he personally stayed with a core force, he could hold William back while reassembling an army.

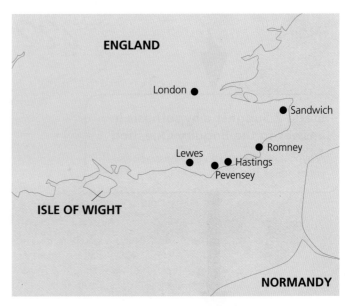

▲ This map shows places in the south of England mentioned on this page and later in this chapter.

4.2 The Battles of Gate Fulford and Stamford Bridge

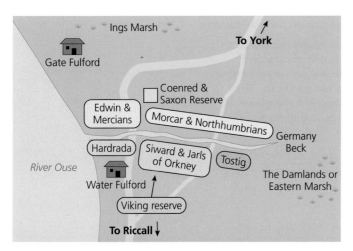

▲ A plan of the site of the Battle of Gate Fulford showing likely troop positions, although we cannot be certain about exact positions.

The Battle of Gate Fulford, 20 September, 1066

In mid-September, King Harald Hardrada of Norway and Tostig sailed up the River Humber then landed and set up camp in Riccall, south of York. King Harold of England was in the south, ready to prevent an invasion by William of Normandy, but a chain of beacon fires may have warned him of the Norwegian landing. Sources suggest he made the decision to march north on 18 September.

Meanwhile, the Earls of Mercia and Northumbria, Edwin and Morcar, rallied an army of between 4,500 and 6,000 men and marched to block the road between Riccall and York. They formed a defensive shield wall on high ground on the north side of a ford that ran between the villages of Gate Fulford and Water Fulford (today this ford is called Germany Beck). The Earls chose this point as the strongest defensive position: the ford was 400 metres wide, a marsh lay to the east and the River Ouse lay to the west, meaning the Saxons' flanks were protected.

Hardrada's army consisted of around 6,000 to 7,500 men. On Wednesday 20 September 1066, the troops clashed. The Saxons initially had the advantage, pushing many of Hardrada's troops on the right into the marshland. However, Hardrada's troops in the centre attacked hard and they managed to cross the ford and push up the banks, driving the Saxons back. Hardrada also ordered troops to outflank the Saxons, probably using an old Roman road which crossed the marsh several hundred metres to the east of the ford. Hardrada's forces then drove the English troops back: some drowned in the River Ouse and others were killed in the marsh. The survivors fled to the safety of the walls of York. Edwin and Morcar survived, but the armies of Northumbria and Mercia had been virtually destroyed.

York seems to have surrendered to the Viking army, recognising Harald Hardrada as their King and promising to help him against King Harold of England. However, rather than occupy York, Harald Hardrada returned to his camp and ships at Riccall. Hardrada's next step was to meet the leaders of the people of York near the village of Stamford Bridge. The people of York agreed to hand over hostages, soldiers and money. Hardrada planned to use these in his next battle for the throne.

The Battle of Stamford Bridge, 25 September, 1066

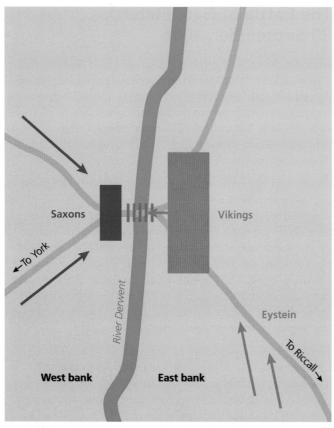

▲ The positions of the armies as the battle of Stamford Bridge began.

▲ An artist's impression of soldiers at Stamford Bridge. Men wore different armour (if they had any at all) and fought with different weapons depending on their status and experience.

On Monday 25 September, Hardrada set out for Stamford Bridge to wait for hostages, soldiers and tribute (wealth given as a sign of allegiance) from the city of York. What happened next was described 170 years later by an Icelandic historian called Snorri Sturluson, who based his account on information handed down through the generations:

> The weather was exceptionally fine, with warm sunshine; so the troops left their armour behind and went ashore with only their shields, helmets and spears, and swords. A number of them had bows and arrows. They were all feeling very carefree. But as they approached the town they saw a large force riding to meet them. They could see the cloud of dust raised by the horses' hooves, and below it the gleam of handsome shields and white coats of mail. King Harald Hardrada halted his troops and summoned Earl Tostig, and asked him what this army could be.

The answer was that it was King Harold's English army. King Harold and his army had ridden and marched north remarkably quickly, covering 190 miles in about five days. Suddenly Hardrada had to organise his men, sending riders back to Riccall to gather all his troops as quickly as possible.

We don't have evidence about how big each army was, but neither was likely to be large: Hardrada had lost many men at Gate Fulford, and King Harold had moved north too quickly to gather a large army. Furthermore, many men of the Northumbrian and Mercian armies (led by Edwin and Morcar) lay dead at Gate Fulford. But King Harold had the advantage of surprising Hardrada.

The battle begins

Most of Hardrada's army was on the east bank of the River Derwent, but still had to arm and form up into their battle order on higher ground. Therefore, a group of Norwegians on the west bank were ordered to guard a wooden bridge to stop the Saxons crossing the river until Hardrada's main force on the east bank had armed and formed up. King Harold easily cut down these men on the west bank and pushed forward to the bridge. Here they were met by a single Viking, guarding the bridge. As the bridge was narrow the warrior was able to defend his position until a Saxon soldier got beneath the bridge and thrust up with his spear, killing the Viking and allowing the Saxons to flood across the bridge. As the Saxons streamed across the bridge, the Vikings grouped into a circle or triangle, the most effective defensive formation. King Harold and a group of men moved forward with a message: Tostig could have Northumbria and a third of the kingdom if he submitted. Hardrada could have 'seven feet of English earth' – implying he would have just enough to bury him in! Both refused.

The Norwegian army opened fire with archers and javelins but it quickly became a savage hand-to-hand battle, with the Saxons trying to break up the Viking defensive formation. At some point, Hardrada was killed by an arrow in the windpipe. Harold offered quarter (talks and negotiations), but the Vikings refused as reinforcements had arrived from Riccall, led by Eystein Orre. The Vikings then reportedly fought with berserker rage (a nearly uncontrollable rage) and the Saxons were pushed back. However, the Viking reinforcements began to tire, were pushed back, broken into smaller bands and picked off one by one.

The impact of Stamford Bridge

Stamford Bridge was a momentous victory for Harold. Winning in the north was important as it showed off his power in a region that had troubled kings in the past. Tostig and Hardrada were dead. Harold allowed Hardrada's son, Olaf, to sail away in return for an oath of friendship, promising never to trouble England again. He returned home with just 25 ships of men, out of as many as 300 that had originally landed.

Harold then received devastating news. William had landed in the south and was pillaging land in Wessex to feed his large army. Harold left with orders to Edwin and Morcar to raise a new army and join him in the south. Harold and his men must have been exhausted – and his army had been weakened by wounds and deaths – but they needed to fight at least one more battle to save Harold's crown and save England from conquest.

Skeletons discovered by ▶ archeologists at Riccall where the Norwegian fleet anchored. Scientific tests of the teeth reveal that these people grew up in northern Europe. They are almost certainly the remains of men from Harald Hardrada's army.

4.3 Your enquiry: Why did William win the Battle of Hastings?

Harold's success at Stamford Bridge showed he had great qualities of leadership. If England had not then been invaded by William of Normandy, Harold would probably be remembered as a highly successful soldier and king. However, the Normans did invade and three weeks later Harold lay dead on the battlefield at Hastings. The Norman chroniclers had no doubt why William won at Hastings as William of Poitiers (see page 8) explained:

> Duke William excelled everyone in the battle in bravery and military skill. He dominated this battle, stopping his own men from running, strengthening their courage, sharing their dangers. He asked them to go with him rather than ordered them to go in front of him and led by his valour and gave them courage. At the mere sight of this wonderful knight many of his enemies lost heart even before they received a scratch.

The rest of this chapter explores why William won at Hastings, but also why he did not win easily – Harold and the English army came very close to winning the battle themselves. Was William's leadership really the crucial factor?

On page 33 we explained the enquiry process – you begin with a question and then create a hypothesis. In this chapter the exam question asks you to make your own judgement about why William was victorious:

'The main reason for the Norman victory at the Battle of Hastings was Duke William's leadership.' How far do you agree? Explain your answer.

Now create your own hypothesis by completing the tasks opposite.

Visible learning

Inevitability warning!

Why are you filling in cards about both William and Harold if it was William who won at Hastings? The reason we're asking you to do cards for both men is because it's important that you understand that Harold had many strengths. William's success was far from inevitable.

Creating your hypothesis

1 Create a set of Knowledge Organisers like the one shown below. Give yourself plenty of space so use one side of paper for each one.
   - Harold's leadership
   - Harold's preparation and organisation
   - Harold's army and their weapons
   - Harold's tactics
   - William's leadership during the battle
   - William's preparation and organisation
   - William's army and their weapons
   - William's tactics
   - chance and luck.

Harold's leadership	
Evidence to suggest it was a strength	Evidence to suggest there were problems/issues

2 Now review the battles of Gate Fulford and Stamford Bridge on pages 35–37. What evidence can you add to any of your cards which might be useful in answering your enquiry question.

To get you started, here are some sentences – which Knowledge Organisers should they be written on?

Many men from Mercia and Northumbria were killed at Gate Fulford, so Harold had fewer men to take south to fight William.

Harold won a decisive victory at Stamford Bridge, partly because he took the Norwegians by surprise.

Harold and his army marched nearly 400 miles (190 miles north, 190 miles south) within three weeks so they were certainly tired when they faced William.

3 Use the information on your Knowledge Organisers and your own knowledge (perhaps from Key Stage 3) to write a paragraph answering the question. You do not have to be certain – it is a hypothesis, a first answer.

The Battle of Hastings

THE BATTLE OF HASTINGS

Read pages 39–43. Your task is to find and add evidence to your Knowledge Organisers from page 38 which helps to explain:

1 why William won

2 why Harold was nearly successful.

2   Spring and summer 1066: William had ships built to carry warhorses and his men. He assembled a large army with forces from many parts of France, and kept his men and horses well-fed for over two months whilst they waited to sail. Just to feed his 2,000 horses meant William had to organise 13 tonnes of grain, and 13 tonnes of hay every day (that's 13 BMW Mini Coopers in volume!).

Card 2 is excellent evidence for William's leadership being a strength. Can you explain why?

1   During 1066, William rallied support from his followers and gathered an army, aware that England's military resources were excellent. He secured the backing of Pope Alexander, using propaganda saying that Harold had broken his sacred oath in which he said he would help William become king. The Pope's support meant the invasion was now a holy **crusade**, and that those who took part would be rewarded by God. This encouraged more men to join William.

▼ The Bayeux Tapestry shows William's men preparing for the invasion. Woodmen fell trees and shape them into planks. The planks are used for building boats which men drag down to the sea. Other scenes in the Tapestry show ships being loaded with equipment, food and drink.

3   William's invasion was held up because the wind was blowing against his ships and he could not get out of port. When he did set off, a storm damaged some of his fleet and they had to take shelter in St Valery port. Some of William's men drowned and were buried secretly so as to not destroy morale. This delay put more strain on his resources and there was concern that he would lose support if the invasion could not take place quickly.

4   The wind changed direction. On 27 September William set sail, landing at Pevensey the next day. However, some of William's ships got lost and landed separately in Romney. There English soldiers attacked and slaughtered the crew.

Harold was still in the north so William was able to march his army a few miles inland. He ordered his men to build a motte and bailey castle to protect the army. His men then **pillaged** and **plundered** the local area, hoping to provoke Harold into an early battle.

5   After the battle of Stamford Bridge, Harold received news that William had invaded. He quickly rode south, pausing in London to rest his men and gather new ones, then marched to meet the invaders. Although he did get more men, he did not have as many as he would have done before the Norwegian invasion. Historians think Harold's swift march was to take William by surprise, and also to defend his lands in Wessex, making sure that people regarded him as a king who was keen to protect his country (remember he had only been crowned in January).

?

Some people argue that the details on Card 5 can be used as evidence of Harold's poor leadership. Can you challenge this argument and explain why Card 5 might suggest good leadership?

6   Harold's army did not take the Normans by surprise. It is likely that William's scouts spotted the advancing English army. Instead Harold formed his troops in a strong defensive position on top of a ridge, blocking the road to London. Thick undergrowth and woods on the left and right meant William would not be able to outflank him.

▶ A reconstruction illustration of the Battle of Hastings opening from the English position, by Peter Dunn. Compare this with the Bayeux Tapestry on page 42 and you can see the similarities between the armour and weapons of the two armies.

7   The front line of Harold's troops were well-armed and armoured housecarls, who were full-time, highly experienced soldiers, fighting with axes and swords. They formed a strong shield wall. Behind them were thegns (experienced but part-time soldiers) and the fyrd (ceorls and peasants who mostly had military training). They carried javelins, swords, bows and axes, but there were relatively few archers. Estimates vary, but it is likely that in total Harold had around 6,000 men.

8   William's men were arranged into three divisions – the Bretons on the left, the Normans in the middle with William and the papal banner, and on the right soldiers from France, Picardy, Boulogne and Flanders. Each division had archers, cavalry and infantry. Estimates vary, but it is likely that William had around 7,500 men. Norman sources say that before the battle broke out, William gave a speech to his men reminding them of their abilities and talents as warriors, that they had God's support, and told them of the severe dangers they would face if they lost the battle.

9   The battle began early on 14 October: firing up hill made it difficult for the Norman archers to weaken the Saxon army. William ordered his infantry up the hill: they were met with a hail of missiles: spears, axes, stones, rocks and some arrows. William thus sent his cavalry in. The cavalry charged but the horses were slowed by the hill and damp ground from the bad weather, making it easier for the Saxons to stop them; the Anglo-Saxon axe was powerful enough to slice a horse and its rider! Harold evidently had a significant advantage: William was having to work hard to win before Harold got more reinforcements, whilst Harold was simply having to defend.

10   As the death toll in William's army grew, the Breton army on the left fled in panic. Some Saxon warriors chased the fleeing Bretons. Harold – on foot – could do nothing as he was too far away to give orders. The Bretons turned on them and, as the Bretons were on horseback, they easily slaughtered the Anglo-Saxons.

▲ The Anglo-Saxon soldiers protect themselves with their shield wall, while the Normans attack from both sides.

Is Card 11 evidence of chance and leadership for both Harold and William? If so, can you explain why?

11   Now the Norman troops in the centre and left pulled back from the fight. Rumour spread that William had been killed. The Norman army seemed on the brink of defeat. William saw the disorder: he lifted his helmet and rode through his troops so all might see his face, shouting out that he was alive.

12   At this point (estimated to be between 2–3pm) there was a pause in fighting. This was standard behaviour in medieval warfare: the rules of warfare allowed sides to take on water and food, and collect the dead. Harold still had the high ground and if he could hold it until nightfall (which comes early in October) the Normans would be forced to withdraw and then would be in great danger of being attacked at night, split up and slaughtered.

13   Bitter fighting resumed: but this time William may have ordered his men to pretend to run away in order to trap more Saxon soldiers and break the shield wall. There is evidence that in at least one other battle Norman soldiers had used this tactic of a 'feigned flight' to fool and defeat their enemy. As the afternoon wore on, the shield wall became weaker. Harold's brothers, Gyrth and Leofwine, were killed at some point, but William had still not taken the hill. There was little time left before sunset.

▲ The Bayeux Tapestry also emphasised William's leadership. Here he is shown pushing back his helmet so his men could see he was still alive and to stop them fleeing.

▼ A reconstruction illustration of the feigned flight, by Peter Dunn.

▲ We do not know how Harold died. This famous scene from the Bayeux Tapestry seems to show a soldier with an arrow in his eye, but it is more likely that Harold is the man being cut down by a Norman soldier on horseback.

14   In the late afternoon, perhaps around 4pm, William rallied his soldiers in a last big push to break the Saxon line. His archers fired arrows and the surviving cavalry and infantry charged. Meanwhile, a group of Normans was ordered to focus their efforts on Harold: his position was marked by a banner. He was killed – perhaps by an arrow in the eye, or maybe by Norman knights with swords: accounts vary.

Is Card 14 evidence of chance acting in William's favour or William's leadership – why?

15   With Harold's death, many of the surviving English fled. This meant the Saxon line was that much shorter, and the Normans forced their way onto the hill on the left, outflanking the Saxons. As night came, the battlefield was covered with the blood of the English. Harold's own body was hacked to pieces.

HOW CERTAIN ARE WE ABOUT THE EVENTS OF THE BATTLE?

The Norman sources give long and detailed accounts of the battle but the English accounts are very short indeed. One version of the Anglo-Saxon Chronicle simply says:

> and Harold came from the north and fought with William before all the army had come, and there he fell with his brothers Gyrth and Leofwine and William conquered this country.

Another says:

> King Harold assembled a large army and came against William at the place of the hoary apple tree. And William came against him by surprise before his army was in battle array. But the King fought hard with the men who were willing to support him and there were heavy casualties on both sides. There King Harold was killed and his brothers Leofwine and Gyrth and many good men.

1   Why do you think English accounts of the battle are so much shorter than Norman accounts?

2   What clues can you find in the two quotations above which may suggest why William won?

3   Why do you think historians have to be very careful when using Norman accounts of the battle as evidence?

4.4 Turning points at Hastings

A student chose to turn cards 1–14 from the preceding pages into a success/failure graph for William and Harold (below). You can see that before the Battle of Hastings begins, Harold has a degree of success – which cards reflect this? Likewise, William faced challenges before the battle – which cards reflect this?

Once the battle begins, the student's graph suggests that both Harold and William experienced success, being reasonably matched, and that as late as 3pm, after 6 hours of fighting, it was far from obvious that William would win… But then events took a dramatic turn, never going back to the way they were, and culminating in William defeating Harold. This is shown in the shaded section on the graph. This period contained the turning points of the battle.

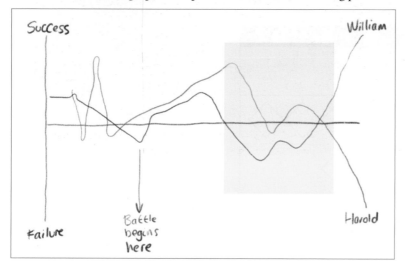

TURNING POINTS

In history, when events take a dramatic turn, we call it a turning point. A turning point can only be a turning point if events continue to change after it. If events don't change, then the event is a milestone: simply a significant or noteworthy event.

DECISON-MAKING **?**

Choose two decisions made by each leader during the battle and explain how successful each decision was.

HASTINGS – THE TURNING POINTS **?**

Go back to the story cards of the Battle of Hastings. Identify what you think were the turning points. You might not choose the same points in time as the student who drew the graph above, and that's ok. The important thing is to decide for yourself how many turning points there were, and why they were turning points.

Turning Point	What happened at this moment and why?	What role (if any) did William's leadership play at this moment?	What were the consequences of the turning point?
1			

Visible learning

How does talking help?

You will probably tackle the Activity above on turning points more effectively if you discuss possible turning points with a friend. This is a good example of an activity when talking helps you do better. Some people think that students are only working effectively if the classroom is quiet. This is wrong. Experience shows that students write better answers if they have first talked through their answer with other people. Talking helps us organise ideas in our minds, choose the right words and decide what evidence we need to prove a point.

Visible learning

Using precise vocabulary about causation

Understanding causation – why things happen – is an important part of being a historian and is essential to your GCSE history work. Historians use words such as 'inevitable', 'likely', 'crucial' or 'turning point' and others to help them explain more accurately the contributions made by each cause or factor to why something happened. Why events happened is always complex, but using the right vocabulary can help you make sense of that complexity and explain it clearly, too.

You can read more about the use of effective vocabulary in the Writing Guide on page 114.

4.5 Communicating your answer

This page helps you write an answer to this question:

'The main reason for the Norman victory at the Battle of Hastings was Duke William's leadership.' How far do you agree? Explain your answer.

The most important task before you begin writing is to decide why you think William won the battle? To do this:

1   Arrange the factor diamonds opposite in a pattern such as the ones shown in the chart. You can have as many factors as you wish in each part of the chart. Use the evidence in your completed Knowledge Organisers and turning points table to help you.

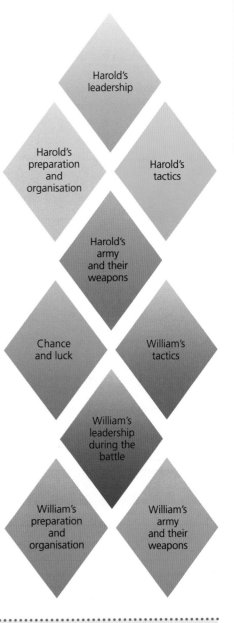

	Example hypothesis A	Example hypothesis B
Factors making William's victory inevitable	◇ ◇	◇
Factors making William's victory probable	◇ ◇ ◇	◇ ◇ ◇ ◇
Factors making William's victory possible	◇ ◇	◇ ◇
Factors that had no part in William's victory	◇ ◇	◇ ◇

Now it's time to write your answer!

You will find more guidance on answering this type of 16-mark examination question on pages 120–121. Remember to develop and use your Word Wall – some suggestions are given below.

motte and bailey castle   Bretons   Papal banner
pillage   favourable wind   hostages   plunder
feigned retreat   shield wall   well-matched
turning point   consequence   impact
uncertainty   hindsight   inevitable   timing
crucial   most influential reason   significant role in

Practice questions

Use the guidance on pages 114–123 to help you write effective answers to these questions.

1   Describe **two** features of:
   a)   the Battle of Stamford Bridge
   b)   William's preparations to invade England
   c)   the Anglo-Saxon army at the Battle of Hastings
   d)   William's leadership at the Battle of Hastings.

2   Explain why King Harold lost the Battle of Hastings.

3   'The main consequence of the Norwegian invasion of England in 1066 was that there was no English army to stop William of Normandy's army landing in England.' How far do you agree? Explain your answer.

How should we remember William of Normandy?

You have now explored William's early life and the campaign which led to his victory at Hastings. This activity gives you the chance to sum up how you see William of Normandy.

Choose **three** of the words from the wall below that you think best describe William or choose other words of your own. For each word explain your choice. You could refer to one or more of the aspects of William's life shown on the right.

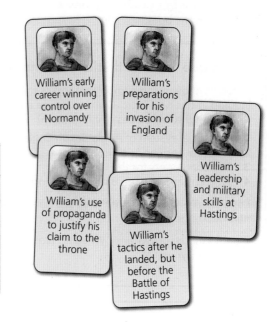

William's early career winning control over Normandy

William's preparations for his invasion of England

William's use of propaganda to justify his claim to the throne

William's tactics after he landed, but before the Battle of Hastings

William's leadership and military skills at Hastings

devious   clever   thoughtful   risk-taking

cunning   lucky   ruthless   vicious   brave

heroic   inspirational   cruel   organised

thorough   meticulous   energetic

self-righteous   well-prepared

Visible learning: Revise and remember

Now that you've finished Key Topic 1, you need to spend time revising. This might sound crazy: you might say you haven't finished the course yet, and that you don't plan to revise until just before your GCSE exams. But that would be a dangerous approach, as the graphs show.

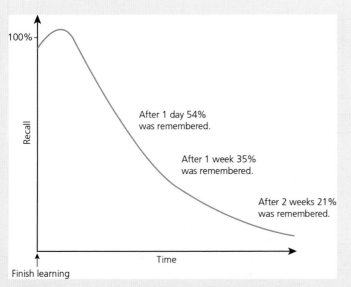

After 1 day 54% was remembered.

After 1 week 35% was remembered.

After 2 weeks 21% was remembered.

▲ Graph 1: The Ebbinghaus Curve of Forgetting. That sounds impressive but the graph is alarming. We forget the detail of what we study very quickly.

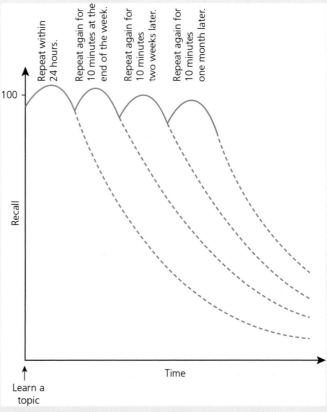

Repeat within 24 hours.

Repeat again for 10 minutes at the end of the week.

Repeat again for 10 minutes two weeks later.

Repeat again for 10 minutes one month later.

Learn a topic

▲ Graph 2: How do you stop yourself forgetting?

Therefore successful students begin planning their revision while they are studying the topic and do not leave revision until close to the exam. These pages help you start that revision process by introducing some effective revision techniques. There will be more to come later in the book!

Technique 1: make it stick – memorable memory activities

There have been some important topics that you've studied in this Key Topic. Can you devise a mnemonic to remember the key pieces of information?

1   The social system of Anglo-Saxon England.
2   What caused the crisis in 1066.
3   The contenders for the throne.
4   Why William won the Battle of Hastings.

For example, which one of the above does this mnemonic help you remember?

Elderly And Happy Granny Wheeled Nonchalantly Humming Hymns

Mnemonics can be really powerful if they create a memorable image in your mind too.

Technique 2: test yourself

You need to work at making your knowledge stick in your brain! The more you recap what you have learned and identify what you're not sure about, the more chance you have of success. Answer these questions, identify what you don't know and repeat the ones you don't know more frequently to begin with.

1 Give two reasons why the Church was important in Anglo-Saxon society.	2 Name the three main earldoms in Anglo-Saxon England.	3 Place the Battles of Hastings, Gate Fulford and Stamford Bridge in chronological order. (add dates for extra marks!)	4 Describe three features of Anglo-Saxon towns.
5 Give two reasons why William said he had the right to be king of England.	6 Where did Emma, Edward the Confessor's Mother, come from?	7 List two reasons why the Anglo-Saxons won the Battle of Stamford Bridge.	8 Describe two features of Harold's career before he became king.
9 List in order of hierarchy the groups of people in Anglo-Saxon society.	10 What titles did Edwin and Morcar hold in 1066?	11 Describe three features of the Anglo-Saxon economy (repeat for government).	12 What did you find hardest to understand in this key topic? How are you going to help yourself to understand it?

Technique 3: set questions yourself

Work in a group of three. Each of you set five revision questions on Key Topic 1 – you may wish to take it a chapter at a time, setting five questions each per chapter. You should include: true/false questions, multiple choice questions, questions that require brief answers and questions that require longer answers. Then ask each other the questions – and make sure you know the answers!

Technique 4: summarising events and telling their stories

Revise the pattern of events during 1066 by describing the events from the perspective of one individual. This helps you recap the story but also demonstrates that different people had different experiences and attitudes to the events that took place. Choose one of the individuals below:

- ■ Earl Morcar ■ An English housecarl who fought at Stamford Bridge and Hastings ■ William of Normandy
- ■ Harald Hardrada's son, Olaf ■ A Norman knight ■ An English villager from near Hastings

The major events of 1066

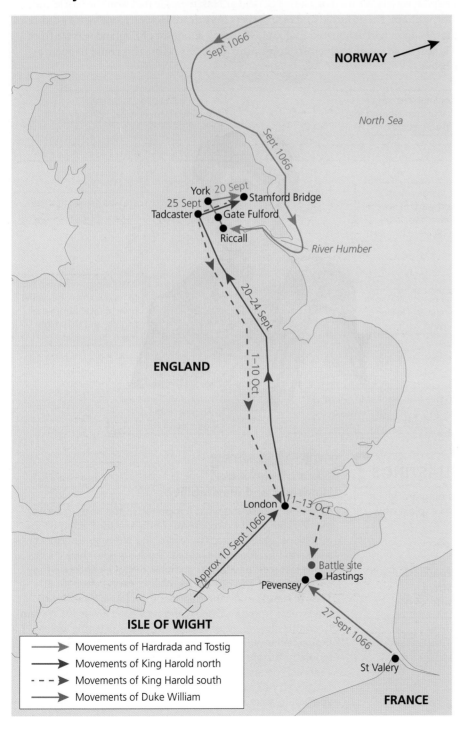

Visible learning

The importance of dates

The events of 1066 show that dates are incredibly important when we study history. Dates don't just tell us when events happened, but how many days there were between events. This is very important in explaining why William won the Battle of Hastings. This is why you need to know the dates of the Battles of Gate Fulford, Stamford Bridge and Hastings and how long it took Harold to march south to fight William. Can you work out why the dates help to explain William's victory?

Chapter 5 William I in power: Securing the kingdom, 1066–87

5.1 William's problems and solutions – an introduction

In the last chapter, we left William on the battlefield at Hastings. He had won the battle and, even better for William, King Harold and his brothers were dead. However, one victory did not mean that William had conquered England. William's conquest of England was far from inevitable. He still faced many problems, dangers and decisions before this could happen, as you can see below.

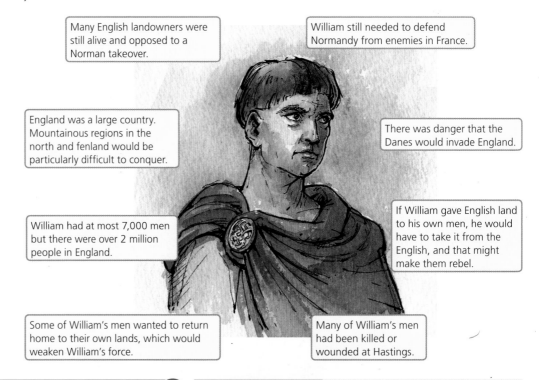

Many English landowners were still alive and opposed to a Norman takeover.

William still needed to defend Normandy from enemies in France.

England was a large country. Mountainous regions in the north and fenland would be particularly difficult to conquer.

There was danger that the Danes would invade England.

William had at most 7,000 men but there were over 2 million people in England.

If William gave English land to his own men, he would have to take it from the English, and that might make them rebel.

Some of William's men wanted to return home to their own lands, which would weaken William's force.

Many of William's men had been killed or wounded at Hastings.

WILLIAM'S PROBLEMS AFTER HASTINGS ?

1 Choose two of William's problems in the diagram which you think would be especially difficult and explain why you have chosen them.

2 Why would William need to be:
   a) very energetic
   b) resilient (able to keep fighting back from difficulties)
   c) careful in dealing with his own supporters
   d) careful in dealing with English landowners?

Visible learning

Hindsight and inevitability

Hindsight – knowing what happened in the end – tells us that William went on to conquer England, defeating all the rebellions against him. Therefore, the Norman Conquest seems to have been inevitable. Students who think the Conquest was inevitable can make mistakes because they underestimate the difficulties William faced after 1066. They underestimate the dangers from English rebellions, the threats from the Danes, and how hard it was for William to control the whole of England with a small army when the fastest way to travel was on horseback. Therefore, ignore hindsight and forget what you know about William's eventual success. If you had been William or one of his Normans, you would often have been worried or fearful – you would have known that success was not inevitable.

Resistance, rebellions and establishing control, 1066–87

This time-chart records the major events in this chapter and how William dealt with rebellions. The questions below start you thinking about how William overcame his problems.

1066 Submission of the earls – English leaders including Edgar Aethling and Earls Edwin and Morcar accepted William as King.

Christmas Day William was crowned in Westminster Abbey.

1067 William returned to Normandy.

Rebellion in Kent.

Rebellion on the border with Wales led by Edric the Wild.

1068 Rebellion in the south-west where Harold's sons attacked the area; rebels in Exeter besieged by Norman forces.

Rebellion in the north by earls Edwin and Morcar, beaten by William's first campaign in the north.

1069 Two major rebellions in the north. A Danish fleet raided the east coast.

William led two campaigns to the north. Two castles built in York at the centre of the rebellion.

Rebellions in the south-west and on the border with Wales.

1070 The Harrying of the North – widespread destruction by William's army as punishment.

1070–1 Hereward the Wake led a rebellion in East Anglia, at the same time as another Danish invasion.

1075 The Revolt of the Earls involved three earls – Ralph, Earl of Norfolk, Roger, Earl of Hereford and Waltheof, Earl of Northumbria.

1076 Earl Waltheof, the last Saxon earl, executed.

1085 A Danish fleet menaced the east coast.

1087 William the Conqueror died.

EVENTS 1066–87

Look at the time-chart of events above.

1 When were rebellions most frequent? (You can choose a group of years, not a single year.)

2 How would you describe the frequency and spread of rebellions in the period you chose?

3 What evidence is there that threats from overseas were continuing?

4 a) List the different methods of winning control that William used.
   b) Can you identify any pattern in William's methods?

2.2 Your enquiry: How did William secure control?

This chapter explores English resistance and rebellions – and also the methods used by William to establish and maintain control of England. You will explore one major enquiry question:

How did William secure control over England?

There are four mini enquiries which contribute to this majoy question:

1 How did William try to control England 1066–67?
2 Why did rebellions break out and then fail?
3 What were the consequences of English resistance 1067–87?
4 Why did the Revolt of the Earls break out in 1075 and then fail?

Keeping track of the major enquiry question

At the end of each mini enquiry you will complete an activity that links back to the major enquiry. You will add notes to the Knowledge Organiser below, identifying William's methods of securing control and the effects of these methods.

Create your Knowledge Organiser on a large piece of paper and use it to summarise the key points. In addition, the individual tasks in this chapter will help you build up more detailed notes on each topic.

William's methods of establishing control in England	Examples or evidence of each method	How did the method help William?	How did the method lead to problems or more problems for William?

DECISION TIME: WILLIAM'S EARLY DECISIONS

Here are three decisions that William faced. What would you advise William to do? Explain the reasons for your advice.

1 Some important English leaders are alive – Edwin, Morcar and Edgar Aethling. Should you:
   a) execute them immediately
   b) imprison them, perhaps in Normandy
   c) let them keep their lands and titles and live as before?

2 What should you do about the two archbishops – Stigand of Canterbury and Aldred of York?
   a) Replace them with Norman bishops and imprison them in monasteries.
   b) Remove Stigand but allow Aldred to remain Archbishop of York so he can crown you as king.
   c) Leave both men as archbishops and have Stigand crown you as king, as he had crowned Harold.

3 How will you treat the English people as you travel towards London? You do not know if Londoners will fight to stop you entering the city.
   a) Treat people leniently and avoid destruction of homes and property.
   b) Order your men to destroy homes, property and farms and kill anyone who opposes you as you head for London.

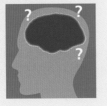

Visible learning

The value of decision-making activities

In Key Topics 2 and 3 you will be asked to take decisions as if you were William or other individuals. These decision-making activities help you learn more effectively:

■ Thinking carefully about which choice to make helps you to understand the situation more thoroughly and helps embed it in your memory. Information has more chance of sticking in your memory if you are interested in and enjoy the task.

■ Thinking about the choices people had helps you understand that choices were difficult and events could have turned out differently. They were not inevitable. This gives you better understanding of the complexity of situations.

REMEMBER: in decision-making activities such as the one above it's not the choice that helps you learn but thinking about and explaining your choice.

5.3 How did William try to control England, 1066–67?

The submission of the earls, 1066

While William and his men were recovering from the battle, the surviving English leaders gathered in London. The earls, Edwin of Mercia and Morcar of Northumberland, arrived with their troops. Edgar Aethling and Archbishop Stigand were also in London. They had to decide whether to resist and fight William. If they did they would need a leader. Stigand proposed Edgar Aethling as king, but Edwin and Morcar turned down the suggestion.

Meanwhile, William did not know if it would be dangerous to launch a direct attack on London. If Londoners and the soldiers in the city resisted, then William was taking a big risk – if he could not capture the city he would look weak and this would encourage more English resistance.

William therefore approached London slowly and took a roundabout, circular route. He first attacked the small town of Romney where some of his ships had come ashore before the battle and his men had been killed. Romney was being punished, but a warning was also being sent to other English towns and people. Then William headed north, then west, crossing the River Thames at Wallingford where he built a castle and moved on to Berkhamsted where he built another castle.

As William's army moved towards London they laid waste to (destroyed) homes, property, crops and farm animals, aiming to spread fear and so intimidate the English into accepting William as king. It worked. First, Archbishop Stigand left London to submit to William as king. He was followed by Edwin, Morcar and Archbishop Aldred, who met William at Berkhamsted. Their surrender is known as the submission of the earls.

William was crowned king in Westminster Abbey on Christmas Day, 1066. Archbishop Aldred placed the crown on William's head. Aldred was chosen because he was highly respected and, unlike Stigand, there were no doubts about his right to be archbishop (see page 31). Holding the ceremony in Westminster Abbey with Aldred officiating was a symbol that William was the rightful heir and successor to Edward the Confessor.

However, the ceremony also showed how anxious the Normans still were. When the people inside the abbey shouted their approval of William's coronation, the Norman guards outside thought the shouts were the beginning of an attack on William. The guards panicked, set fire to nearby houses and fighting broke out in the streets. It was a sign of problems to come.

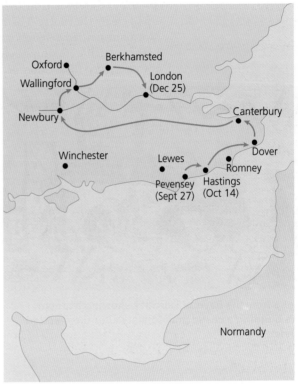

▲ William's route circled London, cutting the city off from reinforcements from the midlands and north. He also took control of important towns – the port of Dover, the religious centre of Canterbury and Winchester, the Anglo-Saxon capital.

THE SUBMISSION OF THE EARLS

1 Why did William not approach and attack London more directly?

2 Identify three tactics William used to intimidate the English.

3 Why do you think the English leaders submitted to William?

4 Why was the submission an important stage in William's conquest?

Castles: reasons, features and importance

William had been building castles since he had first landed in England, as this scene from the Bayeux Tapestry shows. The castle has a low mound (called a motte) with a wooden tower for defence. Many of these motte and bailey castles were built in the first years after 1066, but they took time to build because a great deal of earth had to be dug and built up to create the motte. Therefore, the earliest castles may have been simpler because the Normans needed defences as quickly as possible. They probably built temporary ringwork castles which were simply a fenced area with a bank or ditch sometimes around a simple tower or, even faster, they occupied and fortified the halls of Saxon thegns.

▲ A scene from the Bayeux Tapestry showing Norman soldiers building a castle immediately after they landed in England.

Castles played a major part in William's conquest of England, enabling the Normans to dominate over 2 million English people. They used castles as bases for controlling the local area, riding out to deal with trouble, or retreating into them if attacked. Castles also enabled the Normans to protect their warhorses more effectively. Their horses were a crucial part of their equipment because a knight on horseback, with his shield and chain-mail armour, could cut through enemy foot soldiers. Without their horses, Norman knights had far less of an advantage.

Castles were built on the border with Wales and also on the coast to guard against attacks from the Kings of Scotland or Denmark, but most were in towns where they dominated the largest numbers of people. Castles were so important to the Normans that they destroyed houses to create space for them, even though this risked pushing local people into rebellion. Domesday Book (see page 69) says that 166 houses were destroyed in Lincoln, 98 in Norwich, 51 in Shrewsbury and nearly 300 in York where the Normans built two castles because of the serious rebellions in the region. Much of the building must have been done by local people.

CASTLES ?

1 Why do you think the Normans built:
   a) so many castles in towns?
   b) the first castles out of wood?
   c) most mottes less than five metres high?

2 Identify and explain three important features of early castles.

3 Why were castles so important in conquering England?

Durham

York

Stafford

Ely

London

Hastings

Exeter

◀ This map shows the major castles built by 1100. However, there is no evidence to reveal exactly when each castle was built and historians disagree on how many castles had been built by 1100 – estimates vary between 100 and 500 castles.

▼ A reconstruction drawing (based on archaeological evidence) of the castle built at Totnes in Devon in 1068. Not all motte and bailey castles looked exactly like this because of the space and terrain in which they were built. More evidence is found each year in archaeological digs. Recent discoveries show that some mottes were covered in timber with the timber plastered over to look like stone.

The motte was a mound of earth. Most mottes were not very high. Seventy per cent were less than five metres tall.

Wooden tower – wood was used for speed of building as there was usually a ready supply of timber. Many were later rebuilt using stone.

The bailey was the fenced area around the motte. It would have been full of buildings where the soldiers lived, stored their weapons and stabled their warhorses.

The palisade was a fence which gave protection in case of attacks.

The psychological impact of castles on the English must have been great. They sent out the message that the Normans had taken control and that rebellion was pointless.

Rewarding followers

How do I reward the men who fought for me in battle?

How do I reward my men without provoking the English into rebellion?

It is easy to assume that as soon as William became king he took all the land from English landowners and gave it to his Norman followers. That did not happen. As you read on page 50, William faced many problems and was especially concerned that the English would rebel. Therefore, despite the destruction carried out by his army on their march to London, William tried to avoid provoking the English into rebellion. At first, therefore, William:

- promised to rule within King Edward's laws and to work with the surviving English lords
- allowed Earls Edwin and Morcar to keep their titles and most of their lands as earls
- allowed English thegns to buy back their lands from him provided they had not fought at Hastings
- retained Stigand and Aldred as archbishops and did not replace them with Normans.

These decisions were intended to show the English there was no need to rebel because William was Edward the Confessor's legitimate heir and he was providing continuity to the Anglo-Saxon kings.

However, William did need to reward the men who fought for him at Hastings. He had to show that he was keeping his word to reward them and so was an honourable lord. He also still needed their support to conquer England completely. Therefore, William gave his men the lands of the English landowners who had died at Hastings. For example, King William's boyhood friend, William fitzOsbern, received much of the land held by Harold Godwinson when he had been Earl of Wessex. King William still owned this land but fitzOsbern and the others held their land from him as long as they remained loyal (this is explained more fully on page 70).

The problem of the Marches

The Marches are the borderlands between England and Wales. As you read on page 22, Harold had put an end to disorder and rebellion in Wales in the early 1060s. However, warfare broke out again after Hastings between local Welsh princes. More dangerously for William, these Welsh princes carried out raids into England and were potential allies for English rebels fighting against William.

In order to restore peace in the Marches and defend the border with Wales, King William created three new earldoms. The new earls were men he trusted:

- Hugh d'Avranches, who became the new Earl of Chester.
- Roger of Montgomery, Earl of Shrewsbury.
- William fitzOsbern, Earl of Hereford.

All three men brought peace to their lands, building castles to dominate the areas. They also extended their power into Wales, increasing their own wealth and giving William more security.

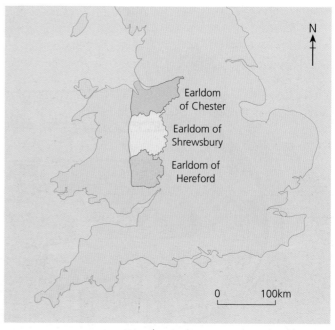

▲ The three new earldoms created by William to take control of the Welsh Marches.

REWARDS AND CONTROL

1 Why did William need to be cautious in distributing English lands to his French supporters?
2 How did he try to retain the loyalty of powerful English landowners?
3 Why were the Marches a danger to William?
4 How did William secure control over the Marches?

William's early success, 1066–67

In the spring of 1067, William returned to Normandy and went on a tour of his duchy to show off his triumph over the English. On this tour William showed off a group of leading Englishmen to his people. In theory, the Earls Edwin and Morcar, Edgar Aethling and Archbishop Stigand were William's guests in Normandy, but in reality they had no choice. It must have been deeply humiliating for them to travel round Normandy, knowing they were there because the English had been beaten in battle by the Normans.

King William left two men in charge of governing England – his half-brother Odo, Bishop of Bayeux, and his good friend, William fitzOsbern. Both men were capable and efficient. They and William must have been cautiously optimistic about the future. So far Norman progress had been successful:

- The English leaders had submitted to William and had supported his coronation.
- There had been no major rebellions.
- The first castles must have over-awed the English who saw them.

However, in the summer of 1067 there was a rebellion in Kent. It was small enough for the garrison of Norman soldiers at Dover to deal with, but it was the first sign of dangers to come. Until now the English had been quiet, traumatised by the shock of defeat at Hastings and the heavy death-toll among the thegns, the local lords. The deaths of King Harold and his brothers had also given the Normans breathing space, depriving the English of the obvious leaders they would need if they were to fight back effectively. However, during 1067, the fight back began.

CONTROLLING ENGLAND, 1066–67

This is the first activity which helps you complete the overall activity for this chapter on page 52.

1 Identify the methods William used to try to establish control over England in 1066–67 (use pages 53–57), then add these to column 1 of your table.

2 Complete the other columns in your table as fully as you can. You can add more examples and information about these methods later in this chapter.

MAKING CONNECTIONS – THINKING BACK AND AHEAD

When you studied history at Key Stage 3 you probably investigated rebellions and protests and why they failed or succeeded. These could have included the 1381 Revolt, the Suffragette Movement or the Russian Revolution. In the next section of this chapter you are going to explore why the English rebellions against William failed.

Think back to your earlier work on rebellions and protests on other topics. What did the English rebels need to be successful and what reasons might explain their failure?

A RECENT DISCOVERY

In 2014 archaeologists uncovered a skeleton in Lewes with six sword wounds on the skull (see photo below). Tests show that the skeleton dates from between 1035 and 1092 which puts 1066 virtually in the centre! This may be the only skeleton providing evidence of fighting in 1066.

5.4 Anglo-Saxon resistance: Causes and outcomes

William returned to England in December 1067. He spent much of the next three years dealing with a surge of rebellions in virtually every part of the country, together with the threat of invasion by Danish forces. This section explores the causes of these rebellions and their outcomes. The map below shows how widespread the rebellions were between 1067 and 1071.

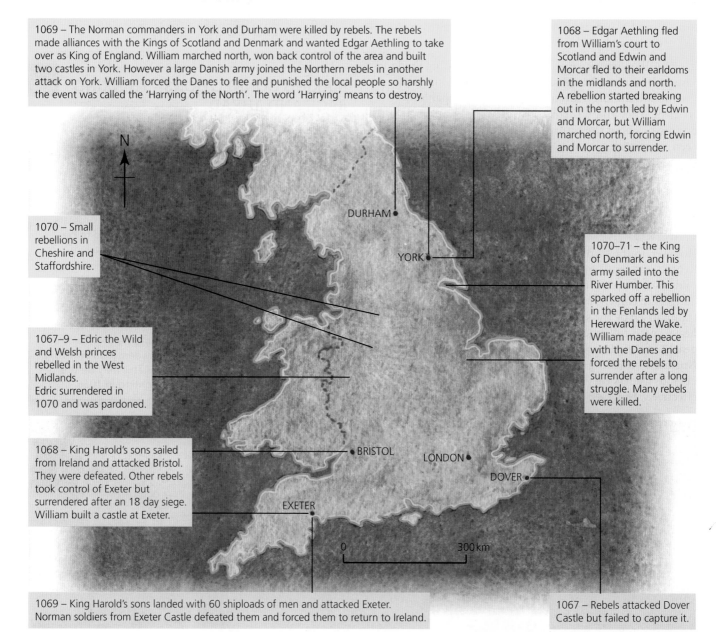

1069 – The Norman commanders in York and Durham were killed by rebels. The rebels made alliances with the Kings of Scotland and Denmark and wanted Edgar Aethling to take over as King of England. William marched north, won back control of the area and built two castles in York. However a large Danish army joined the Northern rebels in another attack on York. William forced the Danes to flee and punished the local people so harshly the event was called the 'Harrying of the North'. The word 'Harrying' means to destroy.

1068 – Edgar Aethling fled from William's court to Scotland and Edwin and Morcar fled to their earldoms in the midlands and north. A rebellion started breaking out in the north led by Edwin and Morcar, but William marched north, forcing Edwin and Morcar to surrender.

1070 – Small rebellions in Cheshire and Staffordshire.

1070–71 – the King of Denmark and his army sailed into the River Humber. This sparked off a rebellion in the Fenlands led by Hereward the Wake. William made peace with the Danes and forced the rebels to surrender after a long struggle. Many rebels were killed.

1067–9 – Edric the Wild and Welsh princes rebelled in the West Midlands. Edric surrendered in 1070 and was pardoned.

1068 – King Harold's sons sailed from Ireland and attacked Bristol. They were defeated. Other rebels took control of Exeter but surrendered after an 18 day siege. William built a castle at Exeter.

DURHAM

YORK

BRISTOL

LONDON

DOVER

EXETER

0   300 km

1069 – King Harold's sons landed with 60 shiploads of men and attacked Exeter. Norman soldiers from Exeter Castle defeated them and forced them to return to Ireland.

1067 – Rebels attacked Dover Castle but failed to capture it.

2016 – IN THE NEWS

In 2016 historians identified the site in Devon of the battle in 1069 between an invading army led by King Harold's sons Godwin and Edmund and Norman soldiers. As many as 3,000 men may have died in this battle.

Your enquiry: Why did rebellions break out and then fail?

This section is not a cliff-hanger with a shock ending! You know all the English rebellions failed so we are not going to try to make the results a surprise. Instead, we will explore why the rebellions failed. You may have begun to think about this already, prompted by the 'Making connections' activity on page 57, but A–E are some outline ideas about the causes of the rebellions' failure.

1 Think about each of causes A–E in turn. Explain in more detail how you think each cause may help to explain the failures.
2 What evidence can you find on the map on page 58 of the effects of each cause?
3 Which cause or causes do you think were probably the most important causes of failure?
4 Which of these causes are similar to the causes of success or failure in other rebellions or protests you have studied?

Collecting evidence for your enquiry

On pages 60–63 you are going to look at three of the English rebellions:

- 1068: The revolt of Earls Edwin and Morcar
- 1069: Edgar Aethling and the rebellions in the north
- 1070–71: Hereward the Wake and rebellion at Ely

These were three very different rebellions but together they help you understand why the English rebellions failed. To assess the reasons for their failure you are going to use the five causes above as criteria. Here are the tasks to complete:

Draw the table below then:

a) Read pages 60–63 about the three rebellions and make notes explaining their failure, selecting evidence to show the impact of the causes.
b) Complete the table showing how important the causes were in the failure of each rebellion. We have modelled this for Hereward's rebellion, but be warned – you may reach different conclusions!

	A There was no strong alternative English leader	B The leadership of the rebellions was poor	C The rebellions were not co-ordinated or lacked support	D The Danes had their own motives and plans	E William's actions and leadership
A fundamental cause of failure	Hereward's rebellion			Hereward's rebellion	
A contributory cause of failure		Hereward's rebellion			Hereward's rebellion
A marginal reason for failure			Hereward's rebellion		
Not relevant to failure					

A There was no strong alternative English king.

B The leadership of the rebellions was poor.

C The rebellions were not co-ordinated and lacked support.

D The Danes had their own motives and plans.

E William's actions and leadership.

The revolt of Earls Edwin and Morcar, 1068

It is actually hard to describe these events as a 'revolt' or 'rebellion'. Very little rebellious activity took place before William headed north to put a rapid end to the plans of Edwin and Morcar.

The sequence of events began when the English leaders fled from William's court. Edgar Aethling went to Scotland, Edwin and Morcar to their lands in the midlands and north. The two earls then began to gather allies against William, including support from Welsh princes who had, in the past, fought alongside Edwin and Morcar's father.

Why did they take the risk of rebelling against William? We do not have their words or thoughts so we have to think about the situation the Earls were in and look at the evidence in Norman chronicles which briefly mention the revolt.

The chronicler, Orderic Vitalis (see page 8), says that Edwin was angry because William had promised that Edwin could marry one of his daughters. This would have given Edwin a lot more status, making him one of the new royal family, but William had not yet kept his promise. This suggests Edwin did not trust William to keep his word in the future. Morcar may have had even more to complain about as William seems to have replaced him as Earl of Northumbria, despite initially allowing him to keep his title. This suggests William did not trust Morcar to defend the north against invasions from the Danes or Scots. William may even have expected Morcar to rebel.

Therefore, Edwin and Morcar had probably realised that they did not have the power they had expected when at first William let them keep their earldoms. It seems likely that they had also been humiliated by being shown off like conquered prisoners when William toured Normandy in triumph in 1067.

William acted quickly as soon as he realised that there was danger. He led an army swiftly northwards, stopping first in Edwin's lands in Mercia where he had castles built at Warwick and Nottingham. Then he headed into Morcar's Northumbria and built another castle in York. Along the way William, according to the Anglo-Saxon Chronicle, 'allowed his men to harry wherever they came', which means that they destroyed housing and crops as a punishment and warning to everyone not to rebel against William.

Edwin and Morcar quickly surrendered without any fighting taking place.

Edgar Aethling and the rebellions in the north, 1069

The rebellions in 1069 were the greatest danger William faced as King of England. There were two outbreaks of rebellion, the second much more dangerous, but they were linked by the involvement of Edgar Aethling, the 'throneworthy' heir of Edward the Confessor, who was now about seventeen years old. We have no evidence from the rebels about why they attacked the Normans. Their reasons must have been a combination of the following:

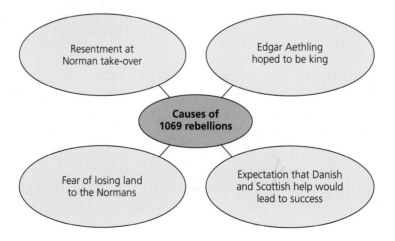

THE REVOLT OF EARLS EDWIN AND MORCAR, 1068

1 Why did Edwin and Morcar plan a revolt in 1068?

2 What actions did William take to end this revolt?

3 Complete your table from page 59, assessing the reasons why this revolt failed. Make sure you make notes to justify your assessment of the importance of each cause.

Rebellion 1: Early 1069

In January 1069 the Normans suffered their greatest shock since Hastings. A Norman army sent to take control of the north was attacked at Durham by local forces. Many Normans were slaughtered in the streets of the town. Their leader, Robert Comyn, was burned to death when he took shelter in the Bishop of Durham's house. The news of the attack gave new life to the angry northerners who resented the Norman take-over. Another English army gathered and advanced on York, laying siege to the new Norman castle. At the same time, Edgar Aethling crossed the border from Scotland and came south to lead this rebellion.

Again William acted with great speed and savagery. He marched his army north, leaving a trail of destruction of homes, farmlands and animals behind him. His arrival broke the siege of the castle and the rebels fled, Edgar heading back to Scotland. William then built a second castle in York and headed south to spend Easter at Winchester. He seemed to have dealt with the problem. He had not!

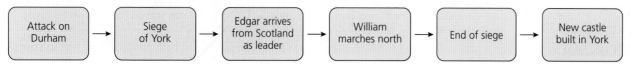

▲ The main events in the first rebellion of 1069.

Rebellion 2: Summer and autumn 1069

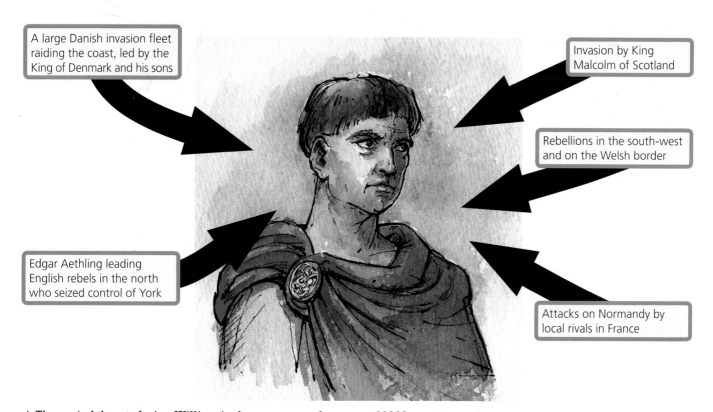

▲ The varied threats facing William in the summer and autumn of 1069.

The diagram above shows why this rebellion was so dangerous. At the heart of the threat was the danger from King Swein of Denmark. In the summer of 1069 a large fleet, perhaps consisting of 240 ships, appeared off the coast of Kent, then sailed northwards up the east coast of England, pillaging and raiding, until it anchored in the River Humber which opened the way to York.

At the same time another rebellion broke out in Yorkshire, perhaps encouraged by the likelihood of Danish support. Edgar Aethling again headed south from Scotland and this time his army seized control of York and its castles, and slaughtered the Norman garrisons.

How William dealt with the threat

William now faced a real threat. The northerners had a strong record of fighting for their independence (as they had against Tostig only four years earlier) and King Malcolm of Scotland might take advantage to try to win control of Northumbria for himself. At that time the border between England and Scotland was not fixed. The Danes might be about to launch a full-scale invasion, a repeat of Hardrada's invasion in 1066.

Therefore, there was the possibility of a very dangerous alliance between Danes, Scots and northern English, headed by an Englishman with a blood claim to be king of England. At the same time William also had to deal with rebellions in the south-west and Wales and attacks on Normandy. If ever he was going to lose England, this was the moment.

William faced the greatest of these threats head-on. For the third time in a year he did what King Harold had done before at Stamford Bridge – he marched his army north at a fast pace and stormed into York. The English fled. The Danes stayed on their ships rather than fight William. William celebrated Christmas 1069 in York where he wore his crown in a great ceremony to show that he was truly king. Around him most of York was in ruins, many houses burned out during the fighting.

William's success was partly based on his own leadership, yet again. He had ruthlessly destroyed opposition and showed immense energy leading his army. However, he had been helped by his enemies. The Scots did not invade England. Edgar Aethling did not lead his army against William. The Danes were not interested in supporting English rebels or helping Edgar become king. They wanted to enrich themselves and, if the chances were good, Swein might have risked an invasion to become king of England himself. However, when Swein brought a fresh fleet to England in spring 1070 he decided he was better off being bribed than fighting and was happy to be bribed by William's gold and sail away.

EDGAR AETHLING AND THE NORTHERN REVOLTS, 1069 ?

1 Draw a diagram to summarise the key event of the second rebellion of 1069. You could model it on the flow-chart on page 61, but you may need a more complex diagram to fit the complexity of the second rebellion.

2 Why was the second revolt in 1069 so dangerous to William?

3 What actions did William take to end this revolt?

4 Complete your table from page 59, assessing the reasons why these revolts failed. Make sure you make notes to justify your assessment of the importance of each cause.

Hereward the Wake and rebellion at Ely, 1070–71

When we study the Norman Conquest it is easy to focus on William and the Normans. They won, William showed great energy and ability, and the Norman chronicles tell us far more about events than do the English sources. However, it is also important to remember how widespread and long-lasting the English resistance was. Time and again English people fought to push back and stop the Norman occupation of England. Even after the defeat of the northern rebellions in 1069 more resistance followed, this time in the marshy fenlands of East Anglia.

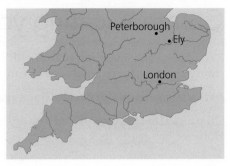

▲ The location of Ely and Peterborough.

Once again the Danes played a part in the rebellion. In spring 1070, King Swein brought a fresh fleet to England, threatening an invasion. The fleet was based around Ely, which today is many miles inland, but was then a large island surrounded by water and marshland and so very difficult to attack. The Isle of Ely became the centre for a number of English rebels, but the man who emerged as their leader was Hereward. He proved an effective resistance leader but could never have won support as king of England.

Support for Hereward

Very little is known about Hereward with any certainty. He may have been a thegn in the area around Ely and Peterborough who lost lands after the Conquest. His most dramatic early act was to lead an attack on Peterborough Abbey whose abbot had been replaced by a Norman called Turold. Hereward, probably with his Danish allies, seized the abbey's treasure of gold, silver and jewelled ornaments, and too it back to the Isle of Ely.

Hereward and his allies held the isle for over a year. At first William relied on his men in the area to deal with the rebels, but they could not overcome the problems posed by the marshland and water defence. Therefore the rebels attracted more support, increasing their threat. In 1071 Morcar joined the rebels at Ely, though his brother Edwin was murdered at around this time. Another danger for William was that it was easy for the Danes to sail up local rivers and along the coast to raid and perhaps trigger other rebellions. English exiles could also easily travel by sea to Ely.

Norman success

Therefore, William decided that he had to deal with this rebellion himself. The Danes were most easily dealt with because they were interested in enriching themselves, not helping an English rebellion. William sent messengers to King Swein offering him money if the Danes would go home. This bribery worked – again! The Danes sailed home with William's money – and the treasures from Peterborough Abbey that had been left in their ships!

William then surrounded the Isle of Ely and ordered his men to build a causeway to cross the marshland, using wood, stones, trees and even inflated cowhides, hoping that his knights could ride across this bridge. However, at their first attempt, the bridge collapsed under the weight and men in chain-mail and horses sank into the marsh and drowned.

A second bridge was made by tying small boats together and covering them with wooden planks. This proved much stronger and William's cavalry crossed on to Ely. In the chaos of the fighting Hereward probably escaped as there is no definite evidence about his fate. Morcar surrendered (yet again) and was imprisoned for life. Some rebels had their hands or feet cut off, others had their eyes put out: William's warning to anyone else considering rebellion.

HEREWARD THE WAKE AND REBELLION AT ELY, 1070–71

1 Why was the Isle of Ely difficult for the Normans to conquer?

2 What role did the Danes play in this revolt?

3 What actions did William take to end this revolt?

4 Complete your table from page 59, assessing the reasons why this revolt failed. Make sure you make notes to justify your assessment of the importance of each cause.

Communicating your answer

Pages 58–63 have investigated the English rebellions against William. You now have enough information to enable you to answer this question:

Explain why the English rebellions against William the Conqueror failed.

On pages 118–119 you will find detailed guidance for answering 'Explain why' questions. However, before you look at those pages, think back to your work so far:

1 Use your completed table from page 59 to organise the cause cards on the right into a pattern to show which causes were most important in the failures. We have included blank cards as a model in the table.

2 Write a paragraph summarising your answer to the question, identifying two or three main causes. This makes sure you have the answer clear in your mind before you begin writing.

3 Plan what sequence you will cover the main causes in your answer.

4 For each cause identify one or two pieces of information that justify your statement that the cause led to failures. In other words:

Don't just say a reason caused the failures, PROVE it.

To do this use your connective phrases such as 'this led to' and 'this resulted in'

WHAT YOU KNOW · · · WHAT THE QUESTION ASKS

Now read pages 118–119 and then you can write a good, full answer!

A There was no strong alternative English king.

B The leadership of the rebellions was poor.

C The rebellions were not co-ordinated and lacked support.

D The Danes had their own motives and plans.

E William's actions and leadership.

A consistent and fundamental cause of the failures		
A contributory and occasional cause of the failures		
A marginal and occasional reason for the failures		
Not relevant to the failures		

Don't forget your Word Wall!

Which words from Chapter 5 so far should you add to your Word Wall?

Practice questions

Use the guidance on pages 114–123 to help you write effective answers to these questions.

1 Describe two features of:
   a) motte and bailey castles
   b) Hereward the Wake's rebellion in 1070–71
   c) William's rewards to his Norman followers.

2 Explain why motte and bailey castles were built throughout England.

3 'The main reason for the defeat of Hereward's rebellion was King William's leadership.' Do you agree? Explain your answer.

5.5 How did William secure control over England? A half-time summary

On page 52 we introduced the enquiry question for this chapter and the table for you to use as a Knowledge Organiser. You began completing the table on page 57 and now you can add more detail, using the work you have done on pages 58–63. The diagram below summarises some of the methods William used to secure control which you can use in your table from page 52.

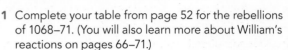

SECURING CONTROL, 1066–1071

1 Complete your table from page 52 for the rebellions of 1068–71. (You will also learn more about William's reactions on pages 66–71.)

2 Which method or methods:
   a) had he used at first but was now using less?
   b) do you think were most important in securing the throne by 1071?

Destruction of whole villages, burning of crops, slaughtering of animals and killing local people if they showed any sign of rebellion or resistance.

Mutilation of rebels – blinding, removing hands and feet.

Castle-building in all towns, on the borders and to guard rivers to make it difficult for Danish invaders to sail inland.

Generosity in allowing English leaders to keep their titles and lands and their freedom.

Imprisonment of leaders of rebellions, especially of English earls.

The **confiscation of lands** and titles from English earls and landowners and giving them to Normans.

DECISION TIME: WILLIAM'S CHOICES AFTER 1069

In 1069 William faced the most serious threats of his reign. Next he had to decide how to deal with the rebels and their leaders. What were the advantages and disadvantages of these actions? Which of these actions would you advise William to take?

1 Building more castles to dominate the population in the north.
2 Ordering his army to carry out widespread destruction of homes and farmland.
3 Pardoning the leaders and many of the rebels.
4 Making an Englishman the Earl of Northumbria, the most rebellious and dangerous region.

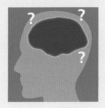

5.6 The legacy of resistance

▲ Nazi troops march through Paris during the Second World War.

Yes, this picture is in the right book. Some of the words used in this section may have reminded you of work you have done on the Second World War and the Nazi invasion of Western Europe – words such as **occupation** and **resistance**.

If you have not already made that comparison between the Nazi occupations and the Norman occupation of England then this page will help you think about it. Can this comparison between the eleventh and twentieth centuries help us understand the Norman Conquest more fully?

Here is the view of Professor Elisabeth van Houts of the University of Cambridge, who published an article 'The Trauma of 1066' in *History Today* in October 1996:

> I wonder whether the insensitivity of modern, mostly English, historians in this respect has something to do with the collective modern inexperience of warfare on English soil? Not having been subject to foreign occupation has de-sensitised the English as to what it means to be governed by people who do not speak your language, settle on your land, force you to pay for land you thought you owned and do all this after having inflicted a humiliating defeat on your people.
>
> As a second generation historian from the Netherlands, which was once occupied by the Germans, I am all too aware of the shock and disbelief experienced by those who were driven from their homes, were addressed in a foreign language, were starved of food, had relatives killed and had to come to terms with this trauma while life continued. Modern experiences can open our eyes to similar events in a distant past as long as we remain aware of the 'otherness' of that past.

THE TRAUMA OF 1066 **?**

1 What does Professor van Houts suggest:
   a) have been the effects of inexperience of warfare on English soil on English historians' views on the Conquest?
   b) about the value of her own family's experience of occupation for understanding the Conquest?

2 What is the meaning of the final sentence in this quotation?

The Harrying of the North

This page explores whether the work of the chroniclers suggests that Professor van Houts' comparison with the Nazi occupation helps us understand the Conquest better. Below are three extracts from chronicles from the early twelfth century 50 years or more after 1066. There was little writing about the Conquest in England in the 30 years after the Conquest. Professor van Houts suggests this is because of the shock suffered by the English as a result of the events, especially those of 1066–71.

Symeon, a monk in Durham in the first decade of the twelfth century wrote:

> It was horrific to behold human corpses decaying in the houses, the streets and the roads, swarming with worms, while they were consuming in corruption with a horrible stench. For no one was left to bury the bodies in the earth, all being killed by the sword or by famine or having left the region on account of the famine. Meanwhile the land was deprived of anyone to farm it for nine years and a great solitude dominated everywhere. There was no village inhabited between York and Durham and they became places where lurked wild beasts and robbers …

John of Worcester, a monk, wrote this between 1124 and 1140.

> After the Danes had invaded, King William assembled an army and hastened to Northumbria. He spent the whole winter laying waste to the countryside, slaughtering the inhabitants and inflicting every sort of evil without pause. As a result a severe famine prevailed. Men were driven to feed on the flesh of horses, dogs, cats and even of human beings.

Orderic Vitalis was born near Shrewsbury in England in 1075. He had an English mother and Norman father. He was sent to live in Normandy when he was a boy. He became a monk in Normandy and wrote his history around 1125.

> King William ordered officers to repair the castles in York. He himself combed the forests and hills, determined to hunt out the enemy hidden there. He killed many people, destroyed the camps of others, harried the land and burned homes to ashes. Nowhere else had William shown such cruelty. He made no effort to restrain his fury and punished the innocent as much as the guilty.

> At the height of his anger he ordered that all the corn and cattle, all farming implements and every sort of provisions and food be collected in piles and set on fire until it was all burnt. Thus was the whole region north of the Humber stripped of everything that could be used to support life. As a result, a terrible famine fell on the humble and defenceless people so that more than 100,000 Christian people, of both sexes, young and old, perished of hunger.

> I have often praised William but I cannot commend him for this act, which killed the innocent as well as the guilty through slow starvation and famine. I would rather describe and pity the sorrows and sufferings of the wretched people than attempt the hopeless task of defending the man who was guilty of such a wholesale massacre. I believe that such barbarous homicide should not pass unpunished.

OCCUPATION AND SLAUGHTER

1 List the methods of destruction described in these sources.

2 Identify at least one example of the vocabulary in each source that shows the horror of the destruction experienced by the English.

3 Which of these sources do you regard as the most reliable account? Explain your choice.

4 Do these sources suggest Professor van Houts' comparison with the Nazi occupation of Western Europe may be a valid one? Explain your answer.

5 Why do you think we have to be careful making comparisons between past and present?

The Harrying of the North: Reasons, features and impact

The sources quoted on page 67 tell us that the north of England suffered horrific destruction at the hands of William's army. This Harrying of the North began in Yorkshire, the centre of the rebellions, then spread north into Durham and Northumberland. Early in 1070 William pushed his army to march across the Pennines in appalling weather (the conditions driving his army close to mutiny), on into Lancashire, Cheshire and down towards the midlands and the Welsh border. The destruction continued and, inevitably, more castles were built, including at Chester and Stafford.

The hallmarks of the Harrying were the burning of homes, the destruction of crops and the killing of farm animals, which put the local people at risk of starvation. It is likely that many local people were also killed, especially if they showed any resistance to the Norman army. Chronicles record refugees from the north begging for food and being cared for at Evesham Abbey in the midlands, which means these refugees had walked at least 160 miles from Yorkshire. Archaeologists have found at least seven hoards of buried coins from this period, evidence of frantic people hiding their wealth before the Normans arrived – and never coming back to reclaim it.

▲ This map shows the region that suffered during the Harrying of the North. The distance between the Rivers Tyne and Humber is roughly 120 miles.

William's motives

When he became king, William did not intend to treat the English in this way. The diagram below shows the likely reasons behind William's change of strategy, although we cannot be certain which reasons were foremost in his mind as we do not have his own words and thoughts.

Frustration at the constant rebellions – just when he thought he had dealt with the latest, another started.

Anger at the failure of English leaders to accept him as king and be grateful that he had left them their lands and titles.

Fear because of the widespread nature of the rebellions and the danger of Danish support for them.

Vengeance for the deaths of his Norman supporters at the hands of the rebels.

To punish the rebels so they would not dare rebel again and so that others would not dare follow in their footsteps.

▼ The Bishophill Hoard from York of 47 silver pennies dating from the very beginning of William's reign. They were probably buried in 1069. Another hoard found in York contains 70 silver coins from the same period and was also hidden in 1069.

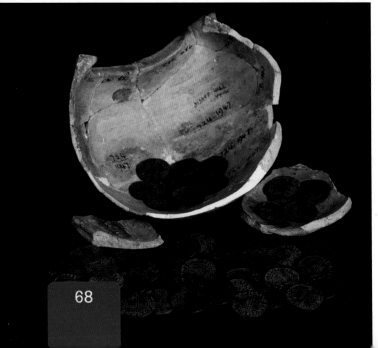

How damaging was the Harrying?

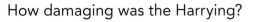

The question in the heading above may seem easy to answer. After all, the sources on page 67 provide plenty of detail, such as:

> … all being killed by the sword or by famine or having left the region on account of the famine. Meanwhile the land was deprived of anyone to farm it for nine years … There was no village inhabited between York and Durham … (Simeon of Durham)

> Thus was the whole region north of the Humber stripped of everything that could be used to support life. (Orderic Vitalis)

In addition, Domesday Book contains very specific evidence which appears to support those descriptions. This extract is one of many from the north, recording the value of lands around Leeds in Yorkshire:

> Garforth. Value before 1066, 60 shillings, now 30 shillings.
>
> Shippen and Sturton. Value before 1066, 80 shillings, now waste.
>
> Leeds. Value before 1066, 120 shillings, now 140 shillings.
>
> Headingley. Value before 1066, 40 shillings, now 4 shillings.
>
> Also Allerton, Great and Little Preston, Swillington, Skelton, Coldcotes, Colton, Austhorpe, Manston, Potterton, Gipton, Parlington are all waste.

With one exception the value of these villages had fallen significantly between 1066 and 1086 when the Domesday Survey was carried out. The word 'waste' suggests there are no houses and no farming taking place, the result of the destruction by William's army. It is possible that the value of Leeds rose because people from other places gathered or were moved there by the local Norman lord, Ilbert de Lacy, and made it a larger, more populated village than before.

This evidence explains why some historians have described the Harrying as genocide. Richard Muir in *The Lost Villages of England* writes of the Harrying as 'the most fearful genocide in the history of England'.

However other historians, such as Professor David Palliser of the University of York, have suggested that chroniclers such as Simeon and even Domesday Book (see page 54) exaggerated the destruction. These historians have asked:

- Wouldn't many villages have been resettled in the sixteen years between the Harrying and Domesday Book?
- Could some of the damage have been done by Scots who often raided the north after 1070?
- Was William's army really large enough to destroy every 'village inhabited between York and Durham …'?
- Why are the places recorded as waste in Domesday Book mostly in hill country which would have had fewer people, and not in well-populated farming areas?
- Does 'waste' really mean there are no people or farming in a village or just that conditions are so chaotic that the Domesday officials could not work out the value of the land?

In 1993 Professor Palliser wrote in an article in the historical journal *Northern History* that:

> the chroniclers may have amplified and exaggerated the atrocity stories … but it was clearly a harrying that shocked men of the twelfth century and struck them as beyond normal or acceptable limits.

This seems a fair and just conclusion. The chroniclers quoted on page 67 may well have exaggerated the exact impact of the Harrying (such as the complete absence of villages in such a huge area). However, they did succeed in capturing the shock and horror people felt at the devastating destruction. It is the chroniclers who do most in Professor van Houts' words to 'open our eyes' to the trauma of the Harrying.

The short and long-term effects of the Harrying	
Short-term effects	**Long-term effects**
Fear amongst the English	Greatly reduced the chances of further rebellion
Many deaths amongst rebels and local people	Confirmed Norman control of the north
Destruction of homes, farm animals and equipment	Led to more castle-building
Refugees fled as far as the Midlands	Increased Norman landownership in the north

THE HARRYING OF THE NORTH

1 How widespread was the Harrying?

2 What do you think the following tell us about the Harrying?
   a) Refugees fleeing as far as Evesham in the midlands.
   b) Archaeologists' find of coin hoards.

3 Which reasons for the Harrying suggest William acted:
   a) in anger
   b) in cold blood?

4 Explain in your own words two reasons why Domesday Book may exaggerate the impact of the Harrying?

5 Do you agree that the chronicles provide valuable evidence about the Harrying? Explain your answer.

Changes in landownership from Anglo-Saxon to Norman

We explained on page 56 that William did not immediately deprive English landowners of their land and give it to his own supporters. However, after the rebellions of 1069, he changed his policy dramatically, as these words sum up:

| ~~Continuity with the reign of Edward the Confessor~~ | ~~Co-operation between Normans and English~~ | **1069** | Destruction of English landowning class ✓ | Replacement of English with Norman and French landowners ✓ |

The evidence in Domesday Book.

We know a great deal about who held the land in England because in 1085 William ordered that a vast amount of information be collected and written up in Domesday Book. You will read more about Domesday Book on page 92, but the important point here is that it records who held every piece of land in almost the whole of England. The king owned the land, but he gave much of it to his supporters to 'hold' as long as they remained loyal to him.

Domesday Book is organised by counties and each county entry begins with a list of the tenants-in-chief, the men who held land from the king. It then details every village or area each man owned – and who had held it from King Edward in 1066. This means we can identify the former English owners of land and who then held it in 1085. Here are some of the things Domesday Book tells us about changes in land ownership:

1 In 1066 there had been around 5,000 English thegns who held land. By 1085 they had almost all lost their land. Many now worked for Norman lords.

2 25 per cent of the land in England was held by just ten great Norman barons. For example, Earl Hugh of Chester had an income of £800 a year, which made him one of the multi-millionaires of the time.

3 King William held twice as much land as everyone else put together! His income from his land was £12,600 a year. Next came his brother Bishop Odo with £3,000 and then the great barons such as Earl Hugh of Chester.

4 In 1085 there were 1,000 tenants-in-chief – the major landowners. Only 13 of them were English.

5 The huge and powerful English earldoms of Wessex, Mercia and Northumbria disappeared. There were new earldoms (such as the Marcher earldoms) but they were smaller and so the earls were less powerful and so could not challenge William.

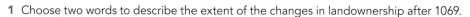

CHANGES IN LANDOWNERSHIP

1 Choose two words to describe the extent of the changes in landownership after 1069.
2 **a)** How did William change his policy towards landownership in 1069?
  b) Choose two pieces of evidence to illustrate this change in policy.
3 Why did William change his policy towards landownership in 1069?
4 Describe two ways in which William's changes to landowning made him much more powerful than Edward the Confessor.

How William maintained power after the rebellions

After 1072 William spent 80 per cent of his time in Normandy. This was probably simply because he was more comfortable in Normandy among his own people who spoke his language. William did try to learn to speak English but did not succeed – after all he had plenty of servants to translate for him! However, the fact that he spent so little time in England suggests that the dangers from rebellions had faded significantly. There was one more revolt in 1075 but that, as you will read on page 72, involved very few English people. Evidence of a change taking place could be seen in William's army fighting in France in 1073 – it had a large contingent of English soldiers.

as you will read on page 72

OVERCOMING RESISTANCE, 1068–1071

This page summarises William's methods of securing his hold over England in the aftermath of the English resistance between 1068 and 1071.

1 Complete your table from page 52, adding evidence of the methods William used to overcome resistance from pages 66–70.

2 Which method or methods played the greatest part in increasing his security at this time?

Mutilation of rebels – blinding, removing hands and feet.

Destruction of whole villages in the Harrying of the North, which involved the burning of crops, slaughtering of animals and killing local people if they showed any sign of rebellion or resistance.

Imprisonment of leaders of rebellions, especially of English earls such as Morcar.

Confiscating lands and titles from English earls and landowners and giving them to Normans.

Castle-building throughout England, in all towns, on the borders and guarding rivers to prevent Danish invaders sailing inland. Two castles were built in York which had been a constant trouble-spot.

▲ In the 1070s William began the building in stone of the White Tower. The White Tower soon dominated London and symbolised Norman power.

5.7 The Revolt of the Earls, 1075

That was the bridal feast, alas,

Through which death to many came to pass.

The above two lines from the Anglo-Saxon Chronicle introduce the Revolt of the Earls, by far the strangest of the rebellions against William the Conqueror. Even the planning was strange because it happened at a bridal feast, the meal after a wedding, when you would expect people to focus on eating, drinking and dancing, not planning rebellion and the death of the king.

What was even stranger was the identity of the plotters. The wedding united two of the leading French families who, until then, had been among William's closest supporters. However, now they became the king's sworn enemies. The diagram below shows the three men who took part in the plot:

The Plotters

The bride's brother: Roger, Earl of Hereford, son of William fitzOsbern

The bride: Emma fitzOsbern, daughter of King William's old friend William fitzOsbern

The new husband: Ralph, Earl of Norfolk

The honoured guest: Waltheof, Earl of Northumbria, an Englishman

The reasons for the revolt

The exact reasons that motivated each man are not known because we do not have their words in letters or other documents, but historians have looked at their careers and these are their conclusions:

Roger, Earl of Hereford

Roger was the son of King William's old friend, William fitzOsbern, who had played a major part in the invasion and conquest and was King William's most trusted supporter until his death in 1071. Roger inherited some of his father's lands but resented that he was given far less power and land than his father.

Ralph, Earl of Norfolk

His family came from Brittany and he and his father fought for William at Hastings. His father died around 1069 and Ralph inherited most of his lands and titles. In 1069 he defended Norwich against a Danish attack. However, he seems to have resented that King William had not given him as much power as his father had had.

Waltheof, Earl of Northumbria

Waltheof was the last English earl. Aged sixteen, he submitted to William in 1066, rebelled in 1069, then submitted again. He was pardoned and married King William's niece, Judith. He was given lands in the south of England and made Earl of Northumbria in 1072. However, he was only given the northern half of the earldom of Northumbria and was much less wealthy than Norman earls.

The plan – and the leaked information!

The rebels' plans were vague and very optimistic. Like other rebels before them, they hoped to get both Danish support and support from English people. They then hoped to defeat William's forces and take over England. Finally they intended to split England into three parts, with Waltheof controlling the north, Roger the west and Ralph the east. One of them would be king, though we do not know if they had decided on who would wear the crown. In practice, it seemed a recipe for further warfare between the three of them, even if they had beaten William's armies.

The one thing that seemed to be in their favour was that King William was in Normandy. However, he had left England in the care of a very capable **regent**, Lanfranc, the Archbishop of Canterbury, who also had the support of William's half-brother, Odo of Bayeux. Lanfranc was also surprisingly well informed because one of the plotters confessed all he knew even before the revolt got underway!

It was Waltheof who betrayed the plot to Lanfranc. The revolt had not begun and Waltheof had certainly not raised his sword in anger when he went to see Lanfranc and told him all he knew. Again we do not know why Waltheof did this. He may never have been a serious rebel, and immediately regretted talking to Ralph and Roger. It is possible they had forced him to take part in discussions, and he informed Lanfranc as soon as he had the chance. Either way, Lanfranc was forewarned.

▲ This map shows how the plotters may have intended to split up England once they were successful and in control.

THE REASONS FOR THE REVOLT

Explain the motives of the three earls who planned the revolt.

The defeat of the revolt

Once he knew of the plot, Lanfranc tried to stop rebellion and warfare breaking out. He wrote letters to Roger of Hereford, trying to persuade him to make peace with King William who, after all, had so trusted Roger's father. Roger and Ralph did not back down. They led their armies towards each other, planning to meet up and march south. However, Lanfranc sent two royal armies north which came between the rebel armies and stopped them combining. The hoped-for Danish support did arrive, but long after the rebels had fled or been captured. The Danes **pillaged** York again and then sailed home. As usual they had got what they wanted without risking a battle.

The story of the rebels continues on the next page but, first, think about the decision below.

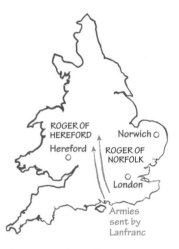

▲ The rebel armies never had the chance to combine because of the arrival of royal forces.

DECISION TIME: WALTHEOF'S PUNISHMENT

King William ordered the imprisonment of Earl Waltheof, even though Waltheof had provided information about the revolt. King William then had to decide if he would punish Waltheof and, if so, what the punishment would be. What would you have chosen if you had been in William's boots?

1 Set Waltheof free as he had revealed the plot (and he is your niece's husband).

2 Imprison Waltheof for life, as you have done Earl Morcar, who also took part in more than one rebellion.

3 Order Waltheof's execution, though you have not previously executed any of the English leaders who rebelled.

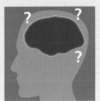

The fates of the leaders

- **Ralph of Norfolk** was cornered by the royal army. Some of his men were captured but Ralph managed to flee to Norwich, then overseas to Brittany, leaving his wife, Emma, to defend Norwich castle against the king's army. Eventually she surrendered but negotiated safe passage for herself and her men to join Ralph in Brittany. The men who had been captured earlier suffered blinding and mutilation as a warning to others not to rebel against King William. You can find out what happened to Ralph and Emma later on page 112.
- **Roger of Hereford** was captured. All his lands were taken by the king and granted to others and Roger was imprisoned for the rest of his life, dying some time after 1087.
- **Waltheof** was put on trial, but it was many months before William decided on the punishment. Then one morning in May 1076, Waltheof was taken out of prison and hurriedly executed by beheading. Initially his body was thrown into a ditch, but at his wife's request his body was retrieved and buried in a monastery.

We do not know why King William decided to execute Waltheof when he had not executed any other English leaders. Perhaps he was angry that the man who had married into his family had betrayed him. Perhaps he had finally lost patience with English rebels. Whatever the reason, the last English earl had lost his title, his lands and his life.

Why did the revolt of 1075 fail?

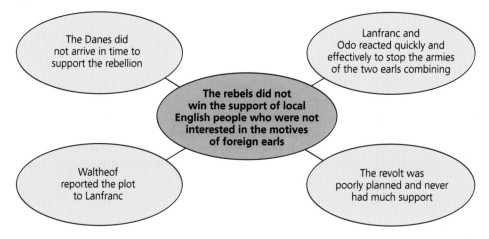

The Danes did not arrive in time to support the rebellion

Lanfranc and Odo reacted quickly and effectively to stop the armies of the two earls combining

The rebels did not win the support of local English people who were not interested in the motives of foreign earls

Waltheof reported the plot to Lanfranc

The revolt was poorly planned and never had much support

The effects of the 1075 revolt

The effects of the 1075 Revolt were actually quite limited. It confirmed what most people already knew – that William I had taken a strong grip on England. There would be no more rebellions while William was alive. More dramatically the last Anglo-Saxon earl had lost his lands and his life. Now there were no Englishmen left who held large areas of land in England. Perhaps this was the moment when the Norman Conquest was complete.

SECURING CONTROL, 1075

1 List the reasons why this revolt failed.
2 Complete your table from page 52 for the revolt of 1075.

5.8 Completing your enquiry

You should have now completed your table from page 52 identifying the methods William used to secure control between 1066 and 1075. You will also have a list of examples of these methods – the actions that he took in the aftermath of the rebellions. This means you should be well prepared to tackle this question:

'The main reason William I was able to keep control of England in the years 1066–75 was the building of castles.' How far do you agree? Explain your answer.

The most important task before you begin writing is to make sure you are clear on your answer. Do you agree that castle-building was the main reason? What other reasons contributed to William's control? Use the activity below to decide on **your** answer.

Where would you place each of the cards below in this table? Make sure you use the evidence collected in your table from page 52 to support your judgements.

Most crucial reason or reasons for William keeping control	
Major reason or reasons which contributed substantially to William keeping control	
Supporting reason or reasons which played a smaller part in William keeping control	

Castles dominated towns and many strategic positions. Their design and their garrisons made them hard to attack.

The Danes often seemed to be a threat but never provided effective support for rebels.

William's ferocious punishments were a warning against further rebellions.

The rebellions were not co-ordinated and poorly led.

There was no strong English candidate as an alternative king.

The changes in landownership deprived English lords of power and wealth they need to rebel successfully.

Now you can move on to plan your full answer. Use the guidance on page 120 to help you.

Updating your Word Wall

Some of these words will help you with answering the question above but you need to be ready to use any of them in your exam. Which questions in the box below will each word help with?

resilient   submission   aftermath   intimidate   co-ordination   garrisons

motte   bailey   palisade   fenlands   Marches   Marcher earldoms   Harrying

mutilation   occupation   resistance   trauma   famine   psychological impact

confiscation   safe passage   bridal feast   inevitable   domination

Practice questions

Use the guidance on pages 114–123 to help you write effective answers to these questions.

1 Describe two features of:
   a) the Harrying of the North
   b) the Revolt of the Earls of 1075
   c) changes in landownership during William I's reign.
2 Explain why William I ordered the Harrying of the North.
3 Explain why the Revolt of the Earls in 1075 failed.
4 'The main consequence of the Harrying of the North was that there were no more rebellions in the north of England after 1071.' Do you agree? Explain your answer.
5 'The main reason for the failure of the Revolt of the Earls in 1075 was Waltheof's warning to Lanfranc.' How far do you agree? Explain your answer.

Conclusion

How should we remember William of Normandy?

William – the man himself

This activity gives you the chance to sum up how you see William in the light of the events you have studied in Key Topic 2.

Choose **three** of the words from the wall below or choose other words of your own that you think best describe William as you have seen him in Key Topic 2. For each word explain your choice. You could refer to one or more of the aspects of William's life shown on the cards below the Word Wall.

clever   generous   **ferocious**   risk-taking   **lucky**   merciful

ruthless   vicious   brave   frustrated   inspirational   **angry**

heartless   magnificent   **calculating**   energetic

vindictive   **well-prepared**

William's actions on his journey to London after the Battle of Hastings in 1066

William's treatment of English landowners at different stages of his reign

William's punishments of those who rebelled against him

William's destruction of homes and villages during and after rebellions

William's attitudes to rewarding his own supporters

The building of castles and changes in landownership

William's impact on England

On page 9 in Chapter 1 we introduced an activity that sums up William's impact on England. The activity used this set of scales to weigh up William's impact.

Now it's time to repeat that activity using the evidence in Key Topic 2 which has investigated the methods William used to secure his hold on England.

Think back over Chapter 5. Which events, policies or changes to life in England would you place on the set of scales or on the sheet alongside?

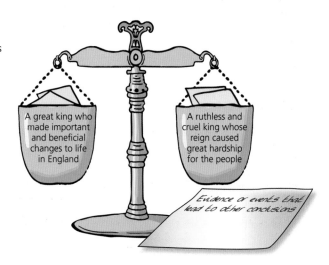

A great king who made important and beneficial changes to life in England

A ruthless and cruel king whose reign caused great hardship for the people

Evidence or events that lead to other conclusions

Visible learning: Revise and remember

Technique 1 Retelling the stories

Retell the story of one of the events in the blue boxes from the perspective of one of the people listed below. You could choose to tell each one from William's viewpoint and then again from the view of someone else.

King William I

Edgar Aethling

Morcar

Bishop Odo

Waltheof

A Norman nobleman

An English villager

Lanfranc

Archbishop Aldred

A Norman soldier

Earl Roger of Hereford

1 The submission of the earls	**2** King William's coronation	**3** The rebellion of 1068	**4** The northern rebellion of 1069
5 The Harrying of the North	**6** The changes in landownership from the English to the Normans	**7** Hereward's revolt	**8** The revolt of the earls in 1075

Technique 2: Test yourself

You need to work at making your knowledge stick in your brain! The more you recap what you have learned and identify **what you're not sure about**, the more chance you have of success. Answer these questions, identify what you don't know and keep repeating this.

1 What was the name of the King of Denmark who raided England in 1069–71?	**2** Name four towns where the Normans built castles.	**3** Which two of King Harold's brothers died at the Battle of Hastings?	**4** Where was Hereward based when he led resistance against the Normans?
5 Name three English leaders who submitted to William in the autumn of 1066.	**6** What were the Marches?	**7** List the three Earls involved in the 1075 revolt.	**8** What were the three new Marcher earldoms called?
9 Who were the losers at the Battles of Gate Fulford and Stamford Bridge?	**10** Who defeated the 1075 Revolt of the Earls on behalf of William?	**11** Why did William allow many English lords to keep their lands and titles at first?	**12** Name two chroniclers who described the Harrying of the North.

Technique 3: What's the question?

We have provided the answers below but it is your job to come up with suitable matching questions. Try to make each question as detailed as possible so you are using your knowledge to help you word it. This is a valuable way of revising because you have to think carefully about topics from a different angle. At least one of the answers relates back to Key Topic 1.

1 Motte and bailey castles	**2** Edgar Aethling	**3** The danger of a Danish invasion	**4** Archbishop Stigand of Canterbury	**5** William the Conqueror
6 The Marcher earldoms	**7** Widespread destruction of homes, crops and animals	**8** A feigned retreat	**9** Resentment because their fathers had held more land	**10** Earl Waltheof

Norman England, 1066–88

A different kind of story

We'd like you to meet an Anglo-Saxon family. They lived in Suffolk in the 1060s and were quite well-off. Leofmaer farmed lands in the villages of Cockfield and Lindsey which he inherited from his father Wulfric. He and his wife, Saegifu, had two children, Adam and Edith. They all had common Anglo-Saxon names. We know about the family from documents drawn up around 1100, probably when Edith became a nun. By then Saegifu was quite elderly.

Leofmaer had died by 1100, perhaps from illness, or in a rebellion. Saegifu had married again. She and her new husband had two sons but their names were very different. Her second husband was Robert, their sons were Fulco and Roger – good Norman names.

So Saegifu was an Englishwoman who married a Norman. What is even more interesting is that her children seem to have got on well together. Adam gave some of the family land to the nunnery to pay for Edith's welfare and documents show that Fulco and Roger agreed to Adam making this gift. They could have objected but they did not – which suggests that they probably got on well.

▲ We do not know what these people looked like but these illustrations may help you conjure up the family in your imagination, to see them as real people. If you had been born a thousand years ago, you could have been one of them.

When Saegifu looked back she must have been very surprised at how her life had turned out. When she was a young mother with her first children, she could never have imagined that one day she would be married to a man from France with sons who had strange French names.

Yet her life *was* changed by the Norman Conquest. She married a man she would never have met if William had not invaded England. Many people had similar stories – their lives were utterly different because of the events of 1066.

Chapters 6 and 7 explore life in England under the Normans between 1066 and 1088. The question we are going to investigate is:

How much did the Normans really change England after 1066?

SAEGIFU AND HER FAMILY

1 What can you learn from Saegifu's story?
2 After 1066, which of these aspects of life in England do you think were:
   a) most likely to change   b) least likely to change?
   Explain your choices.

Medicine	The role of the king	Laws
Farming methods	Houses	Taxes
Religion and the Church	Diet	Language

6 Feudalism, the Church and government

Your enquiry: How did William's needs change England?

William faced threats throughout his reign. There were rebellions in England and attacks on Normandy by local rivals. To deal with these threats William needed the things shown in the Knowledge Organiser table below. In Key Topic 2 you discovered some of the short-term actions he took to achieve these things. This chapter explores other longer-term methods William used to maintain his power. As you read pages 79–93 you can collect examples in this table to build an answer to your enquiry question:

How did William's needs change England?

What did William need to maintain power?	Changes in England – examples of how William achieved his needs
Wealth – he needed to show his power and magnificence	
Strong defences against rebels and invaders	
Control over his people – so they feared his strength and power	
Loyal support to reduce danger from enemies	
Legitimacy to convince people that he was legally king	

THINK BACK AND CONNECT

What examples could you add to this table from the work you did in Key Topic 2?

6.1 The feudal system

We explain 'the feudal system' on page 80. The tasks below lead you into the explanation by exploring the situation William faced when he became king.

William's victory over Harold and the deaths of many English landowners gave William one great advantage. As king he owned all the land in England. However, as you know from Key Topic 2, he still faced threats after he had been crowned. There were rebellions by the English and threats of invasion from the Danes. William therefore still needed an army – he could not let his men all go home or his reign as king of England would be very short.

DECISION TIME: WILLIAM'S ARMY

1 Put yourself on William's throne. How would you make sure you had an army? Choose from one of the three options below. Think carefully about the advantages and disadvantages of your choice.
   a) Keep most of the land in England but give your lords some land to **own** as a reward for their help. Ask them to bring soldiers to fight for your army whenever you need them.
   b) Recruit your army by paying soldiers a weekly wage when you need them. This ensures you only have to pay an army when you really need it.
   c) Keep control of all the land in England yourself but give your lords land to **hold** so long as they agree that in return they will bring a set number of soldiers to fight for you or guard your castles.

2 Two words in the decisions above have been shown in bold – 'own' and 'hold'. What do you think the difference is between them?

The feudal hierarchy

The king

The king owned all the land in England. He gave land to his most important supporters, the tenants-in-chief. They held this land from him. They did not own it themselves.

In return for their land the tenants-in-chief agreed to bring men to fight for the king for forty days a year. The number of men they brought was agreed and set out clearly. The more land a tenant-in-chief had, the more soldiers he brought for the king's army.

Tenants-in-chief

The tenants-in-chief gave land to their knights. This might be a village or villages – enough land to give him enough income to pay for his warhorse, his armour and weapons.

The knights agreed to do military service for their lord, the tenant-in-chief. This was known as knight service. Therefore they made up the quota of knights the tenant-in-chief provided for the king.

Knights

The knights gave most of the land in their villages to the local people, so they could grow their own food. The knights did keep some of the village land for themselves, which was called the demesne (the lord's land). However, as proud soldiers, they did not farm their land themselves. They had villeins to do that for them!

The local people did the work on the demesne two or three days a week in return for the land their lord, the knight, allowed them to have. This work on the lord's land was known as labour service.

Villeins

Many ordinary farmworkers were villeins. This meant they were not free to travel or work wherever they wanted but had to stay and work on the land of their local lord.

THE FEUDAL SYSTEM ❓

1 What did each of these people do for the person above them in the feudal system?
   a) The tenants-in-chief   b) The knights   c) The villeins

2 What did each of these people do for the person below them in the feudal system?
   a) The king   b) The tenants-in-chief   c) The knights

3 Who did each of these activities and why did he do them?
   a) Homage   b) Knight service   c) Labour service

4 What was forfeiture and why was land forfeit?

5 What examples can you add to your table (see page 79) to show how feudalism met William's needs and so helped him maintain his power over England?

The king and the tenants-in-chief

The aim of the feudal system was to provide King William with an army to defend his conquest of England. Victory at Hastings meant that William took over the land of all the English landowners. From now on the king owned all the land in country. In order to raise his army William gave large areas of land to his closest supporters but they did not 'own' the land. They were tenants, which means they held the land as long as the king was happy for them to do so. In return for their land they had to perform an act of homage which is shown here.

The tenants-in-chief were the major landholders who held their land directly from the king – there was no middle-man. They included the king's half-brothers, Robert and Odo, and the great earls. They also included the bishops and abbots because the Church was a major landholder. Historians have calculated that the most powerful eleven tenants-in-chief held 25 per cent of the land in England.

When a tenant-in-chief died, his son did not automatically inherit the land because it was the king's land. Usually the king did give the land to the heir, but the heir had to perform the act of homage and pay the king a tax.

In return, the tenants-in-chief brought knights to serve in the king's army and to garrison the king's castles for 40 days a year. All together, the number of knights from all the tenants-in-chief raised around 4,000–5,000 knights. This was a far more reliable and faster way of raising forces than trying to recruit mercenaries (soldiers who fought for money). That would have taken far longer and have used up a high percentage of the coins in the country!

This 'system' worked well so long as the tenants-in-chief remained loyal to the king and brought their knights to fight for him. If they rebelled or failed to deliver their side of the agreement then they knew that the penalty was forfeiture – their land would be forfeit, which means the king took it back.

Knight service and labour service

The land the knight was given by his lord was held in exactly the same way as the tenants-in-chief held land from the king. The knight had to do homage to his lord and agree to do knight service, which meant to serve him as a knight for forty days a year. In addition, the knight could spend other parts of the year living in their lord's household where they received food and payment. The land the knight held was known as a fief, or 'feodum' in Latin, which is where the term 'feudal system' comes from.

At the bottom of the system were the ordinary people, the villeins, who worked on the land, growing food. Their labour service was to work on their lord's demesne land for two or even three days a week, making sure his land grew enough food to feed the lord, his family and their servants. The rest of the week they could work on the land they received in return for their labour service.

I become your man from this day forward, of life and limb and earthly worship, and unto you I shall be true and faithful and shall hold faith for the lands I hold from you.

▲ A tenant-in-chief performing homage to his king.

DECISION TIME: WILLIAM AND THE CHURCH

On pages 82–85 you will investigate whether William changed the Church in England. If you had been William, which of these four actions would you have taken? Explain why you would or would not have taken them.

1 Accuse the leaders of the English Church of being corrupt and more interested in wealth than religion.

2 Replace all English bishops and abbots with Frenchmen.

3 Support the rebuilding of English cathedrals to make them larger and more splendid.

4 Support reforms to the Church to make it more religious.

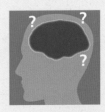

6.2 The Normans and the Church

Visible learning

The bingo card

The bingo card may not look like serious work, but it helps you concentrate on reading by adding urgency and a sense of competition – and you still have to get all the correct answers and record them in your notes so you can re-use them for revision.

William and religion

William was deeply religious. He founded the magnificent St Stephen's Cathedral in Caen in Normandy and Battle Abbey in Sussex so that, according to the Battle Abbey Chronicle, 'the good works of the monks would pay for the bloodshed' of the battle. William controlled the Church in Normandy very closely. He appointed his half-brother, Odo, bishop of the important town of Bayeux, to increase his own control of the town. William also supported the Pope's reforms across Europe to make bishops and priests more religious and better educated and less interested in power and wealth.

The role of the Anglo-Saxon Church

The English Church was a very powerful and wealthy organisation. It owned 25 per cent of the land in England and the archbishops and bishops were often royal advisers. The Church also played an important part in everyone's life in villages and towns and the bishops and priests greatly influenced people's thinking. The Church's role in society – its power and influence – therefore made it important for William to control the Church and also use its power to control England.

Even before he was king, William aimed to control the Church. He won the support of the Pope for his invasion of England by saying that when he was king he would reform the Anglo-Saxon Church to end its corruption. He said its bishops and priests were far more interested in wealth and power than in serving God and the people.

Historians say that William was exaggerating this corruption. There were signs that the Pope's reforms were beginning in England before 1066. However, it was easy for William to claim that the English Church was corrupt because its head, Archbishop Stigand, was living proof that William's accusations were correct.

The corruption of Archbishop Stigand

By 1066, Stigand was over 70 years old, and still extremely powerful. He had been a royal adviser for decades, but the Pope had criticised him for two things:

1 Breaking Church laws by keeping hold of his post and income as Bishop of Winchester after he was made Archbishop of Canterbury. Church law said a man could only hold one **bishopric**. Stigand had two – the two wealthiest in England.

2 Supporting a rival Pope to the official Pope in Rome and carrying out the duties of an archbishop when he had not been appointed by the official Pope.

These accusations made it easy for William to portray the whole English Church as corrupt. If its leader was corrupt then the whole Church must be rotten!

This was also why William was crowned by Archbishop Aldred of York, a deeply religious man. Therefore, there were no doubts that William had been legally crowned king.

◀ This is one of the most crucial scenes in the Bayeux Tapestry. Archbishop Stigand stands behind Harold, implying that he had crowned Harold king. This was important Norman propaganda because the Pope had said that Stigand was not the true Archbishop. This made Harold's coronation unlawful. However, one English writer, John of Worcester, said that Harold was crowned by Archbishop Aldred of York. We cannot be completely certain who did crown Harold.

Lanfranc – the new archbishop

In 1070 William arranged for the Pope's Legate – his representative in England – to depose Stigand as archbishop. The new Archbishop of Canterbury was Lanfranc, the abbot of William's great church of St Stephen's in Normandy. William was making a statement by having a Norman as the head of the Church in England – this was a new start for the Church and 'Normanisation' could begin. This meant bringing the Church completely under Norman control and making reforms that brought the English Church into line with the Norman Church. Norman control had not been so obvious while Stigand had been Archbishop.

Lanfranc was 60 years old, a highly educated and deeply religious man. He had begun life as a lawyer, then spent 30 years as a monk and abbot. He never felt at home in England, but was determined to support William. The two men knew each other well and admired each other's qualities.

The arrival of Lanfranc was not the only change. By the end of William's reign the Normanisation of the Church was complete. Every bishop except one (Wulfstan of Worcester) came from Normandy and other parts of France. Thomas of Bayeux, the new Archbishop of York, was a trusted supporter of William, having been his personal chaplain. Normans and Frenchmen also took over as the abbots of the largest English abbeys. By 1086 only three abbeys had English abbots.

William and Lanfranc had completely Normanised the Church. Lanfranc was in complete support of William as king. Lanfranc's attitude was summed up by his statement that:

> I cannot give any orders that contradict the King's instructions.

Lanfranc did support the Pope's reforms, but made sure that the Pope's influence in England did not increase. Lanfranc made it clear to the Pope that the English Church would not accept every instruction from the Pope. He also told the Pope that, as king, William was an independent ruler and did not owe his crown to the Pope. Lanfranc made sure the Pope did not reduce William's power.

Lanfranc also increased his control over the Church by making its organisation more efficient. The diagram shows how he did this.

Lanfranc's control and re-organisation of the Church

Control of the whole English Church
Before 1066 the Archbishops of Canterbury and York had been equal. Lanfranc insisted that he, as Archbishop of Canterbury, was superior and controlled the Church throughout England.

Regular Councils
Lanfranc held regular councils (also called synods) of bishops. Councils had been rare before 1066 but Lanfranc held ten Councils to discuss and impose Church reforms.

Control within bishoprics
Every bishop now had deputies called archdeacons who 'policed' parts of the bishopric, making make sure that priests were carrying out church services and other responsibilities in the right ways. There had been archdeacons before 1066, but they had little power to deal with problems.

Lanfranc's reforms of the Church

Lanfranc was a firm supporter of religious reform. He wanted to stamp out corruption among bishops and priests. The major problems in the Church were as follows:

- **Simony** – the selling of Church posts by bishops and archbishops instead of giving the post to the most religious and best-qualified person.
- **Nepotism** – giving Church posts to friends and family to increase their influence and wealth.
- **Pluralism** – holding more than one Church post. A good example was Stigand being both Bishop of Winchester and Archbishop of Canterbury.
- **Marriage** – all priests were supposed to be single and to live a celibate life so that they put their devotion to God before any personal link. However, many priests were married.

Lanfranc and his bishops worked hard at dealing with problems in the Church even if William had exaggerated them. For example, in 1075 he ordered that no new priest could be married. Village priests were allowed to keep their wives but priests in cathedrals (viewed as a more important role) had to make a choice – give up their post in the Church or give up their wives and lead celibate lives.

There were other changes too:

- **Monasteries** – Lanfranc was a great supporter of monasteries. He increased the number of monasteries in England and the number of monks within them. He also believed it was important for monks to be well educated so they could, in turn, influence and educate those who were not churchmen. He also insisted that monks follow the rules of the monasteries at all times.
- **Church courts** were set up to deal with anyone who committed religious or moral crimes such as adultery and blasphemy. Priests who broke the law were also tried in Church courts instead of the king's courts.
- **Rebuilding the cathedrals** – Lanfranc led the way by rebuilding Canterbury Cathedral, encouraging other bishops to begin the rebuilding of their cathedrals. The new Norman cathedrals were much larger, both taller and wider with more solid pillars. They were much more powerful, commanding buildings, symbolising the power of the new Norman overlords.

▲ The nave of Durham Cathedral, rebuilt by its Norman bishop. The most visible consequence for the Church was the rebuilding of the cathedrals after 1066. They were rebuilt in what is known as the Romanesque style with wide, round-headed arches and zig-zag decorations over arches and on some pillars. You could also argue that this rebuilding of cathedrals was the most significant religious change because it has been the most long-lasting, a change we can still see and enjoy today.

Opposition to religious changes

Changes to long-established English customs caused opposition, even among monks. New Norman services and prayers were disliked by English priests and monks. Norman bishops, including Lanfranc, also removed the relics and bones of English saints from their cathedrals, claiming there was not enough evidence that these saints had lived holy lives. This caused outrage.

The most dramatic incident was at Glastonbury Abbey in 1083 when the Norman abbot, Thurstan, insisted on Norman services and styles of singing in church. The monks protested so much that Thurstan sent his knights into the church where some of them fired arrows at the monks, who were forced to hide under the altar. Then the knights attacked the monks, killing 3 and wounding 18 more. Thurstan was sent back to Normandy but this was not an isolated example. Lanfranc himself had ordered the flogging of a monk who would not accept the new Norman abbot at Canterbury.

THE CONSEQUENCES OF LANFRANC'S WORK

1 Answer the questions in the table below showing the consequences of Lanfranc's work as archbishop.

Impact on Norman control of England	Impact on the Church
Who lost his job and why was this important for William?	Did he make any reforms?
What did Lanfranc's appointment suggest about Norman control?	Was he interested in monasteries?
What other new appointments followed?	How did the system of courts change?
Did Lanfranc increase the Pope's power in England?	What was the impact of his rebuilding of his own cathedral?

2 What examples can you add to your table (see page 79) to show how control of the Church met William's needs and so helped him maintain his power over England?

Which of the choices on page 81 did you get right? If you are not sure, go back and check to make sure you understand what William chose and why.

DECISION TIME: EVERYDAY LIFE

Which of these aspects of daily life do you think William would try to reform and improve? Think about why and how he might want to change any of them and his situation as king after 1066.

1 Farming techniques
2 The system of slavery
3 The quality of housing
4 The quality of people's diet
5 The speed of transport

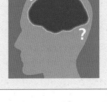

6.3 Everyday life – society and the economy

Society and economy
Society – how people lived and the relations between people.

Economy – how people earned their living (e.g. what kinds of farming and trading took place) and how wealthy the country was.

Life in towns after 1066

In the short term there was destruction in some towns during rebellions. In some towns homes were knocked down to make way for castles. This must have caused a great deal of anger and hardship, but by the end of William's reign in 1087 there had been changes and improvements:

- Towns were growing up around new castles such as Newcastle in the north-east. The castle garrisons bought food, clothing and other goods from local people.
- England was more peaceful after 1071 and it was safer for merchants to travel and trade around the country.
- There were new French communities in towns such as Nottingham and Southampton.
- Ports on the south coast were doing more trade with France because of the new links with Normandy and parts of France. More goods such as tin and especially wool were being sold in France so English merchants made more profit.

King William and the Normans were eager to see trade continuing and increasing. The king collected taxes from merchants so the wealthier they were, the more tax he collected. Trade was good for increasing the king's own wealth.

However, some towns lost out. Before 1066 there had been more trade with Scandinavia from east coast ports and towns such as York. England now had less contact with Scandinavia so there was less trade and this made those towns less wealthy.

Life in villages after 1066

The most obvious change for most villagers was that they had a new lord, from Normandy or another part of France. This must have created a great deal of fear and uncertainty during the early months when a new lord took over a village, not least because villagers could not understand what their new lord was saying. There is no evidence to prove this, but it seems logical that the Norman take-over led to great fear, even if people's daily lives did not, in the end, change a great deal.

Many villages were destroyed or badly damaged by the Norman army as it stamped out rebellions. Many villages in Sussex also suffered in 1066, just after William landed and **pillaged** the area to force Harold into an early battle. Many Saxon landowners now found that they were now having to work for Normans lords – they had lost status and some even became villeins, unfree workers tied to their lord's land.

You can find more information about village life in the illustration opposite.

SLAVERY

One change that might surprise you was the end of slavery. At least ten per cent of the population of Anglo-Saxon England were slaves, but Norman lords did not have slaves and the Norman Church disapproved of slavery. Archbishop Lanfranc told King William to stop slaves being exported from ports such as Bristol. No law was passed to end slavery but Norman lords did not buy slaves, so by 1100 it had virtually died out.

SOCIETY AND THE ECONOMY

1 a) Identify four continuities in English life.
  b) Why do you think these things did not change?

2 Make a copy of the graph opposite. Identify at least five changes in English life. Place them on your copy of the graph and add notes justifying where you have placed them.

3 What examples can you add to your table (see page 79) to show how developments in everyday life met William's needs and so helped him maintain his power over England?

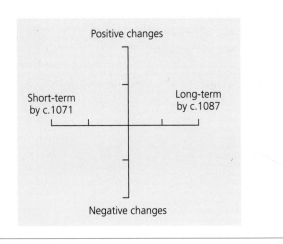

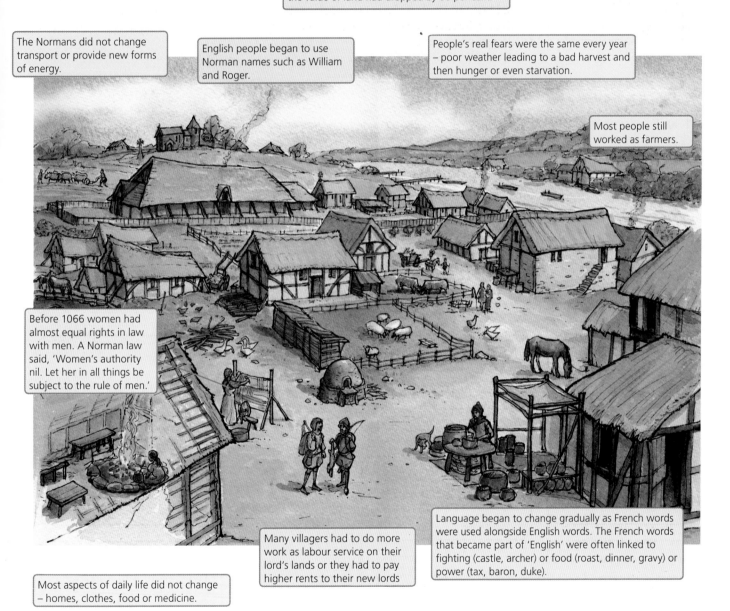

Villages in some areas were destroyed after rebellions. In Yorkshire Domesday Book shows the value of land had dropped by 60 per cent.

The Normans did not change transport or provide new forms of energy.

English people began to use Norman names such as William and Roger.

People's real fears were the same every year – poor weather leading to a bad harvest and then hunger or even starvation.

Most people still worked as farmers.

Before 1066 women had almost equal rights in law with men. A Norman law said, 'Women's authority nil. Let her in all things be subject to the rule of men.'

Language began to change gradually as French words were used alongside English words. The French words that became part of 'English' were often linked to fighting (castle, archer) or food (roast, dinner, gravy) or power (tax, baron, duke).

Many villagers had to do more work as labour service on their lord's lands or they had to pay higher rents to their new lords

Most aspects of daily life did not change – homes, clothes, food or medicine.

6.4 The Norman legal system

One sentence from the Laws of William the Conqueror sums up his approach to the legal system:

> I command that all shall obey the laws of King Edward with the addition of those decrees I have ordained for the welfare of the English people.

First, he wanted continuity because complete change might well lead to anger and then rebellion. However, he also wanted to use the legal system to increase and maintain his power. That was why he made changes when he thought they were needed.

There were two major results of these changes:

1 The power of the king increased. William controlled the legal system throughout the country because he owned all the land.
2 The power of the Church increased because it became more involved in the legal system.

NORMAN LAWS AND PUNISHMENTS

1 a) Read cards A–I below. Each one tells you about an aspect of the Norman legal system. Draw a copy of the scales and put each card letter on the side you think it should go.

2 What evidence is there that:
   a) William wanted to avoid pushing the English people into rebellion
   b) William made changes in response to violence against the Normans
   c) the laws were harsher towards criminals after 1066
   d) the Church played a bigger part in the legal system after 1066?

3 Add examples to your table (see page 79) to show how the Norman legal system met William's needs and so helped him maintain his power over England.

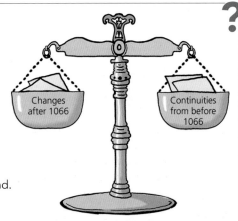

Changes after 1066

Continuities from before 1066

A In some areas there were attacks on individual Norman soldiers. William made a new law that if a Norman was murdered, all the people of that region had to join together and pay a high fine called the Murdrum fine.

B William kept the majority of Saxon laws.

C The Normans kept the system of tithings and the 'hue and cry' because these were effective ways of policing local communities.

D William introduced the Forest Laws (see page 91). Trees could no longer be cut down for fuel or for building and people in forests were forbidden to own dogs or bows and arrows. Those caught hunting deer were punished by having their first two fingers chopped off. If caught a second time, the punishment was blinding.

E The Normans kept the religious ritual of trial by ordeal but also introduced trial by combat. The accused fought with the accuser until one was killed or unable to fight on. The loser was then hanged, as God had judged him to be guilty.

F William used the death penalty for serious crimes and for reoffenders. Executions were carried out in public to show the power of the king. Executions had been rare before 1066 when fines had been paid by the offender to the victim.

G Norman-French became the official language used in court procedures and all court records were kept in Latin. Most English people did not understand either language.

H William used fines for lesser crimes. However, he ordered that fines should no longer be paid to the victim or their family, but to the king's officials.

I The Normans introduced Church courts (see page 84). These were separate courts used for churchmen and tended to be more lenient.

6.5 Norman government

NORMAN GOVERNMENT

1 Read pages 89–93 and answer the questions on each topic. They will help you complete task 2 below.

2 What examples can you add to your table (see page 79) to show how developments in government met William's needs and so helped him maintain his power over England?

The power of the king

Before 1066 the power of the king was high – in theory. Kings had the right to raise an army, make decisions about the Church, decide law cases and make laws and decide how much tax to collect. However, some kings were unsuccessful. They did not have strong enough personalities and gave power away to their earls. In contrast, William was a very strong character who dominated everyone and made sure that no one challenged his power as king. The Anglo-Saxon Chronicle was right when it described him as 'a very stern and violent man. No one dared do anything against his will'.

Therefore William did not need to use new methods to build up his power but used existing methods more efficiently. William was in the centre of all aspects of government and decision-making so this form of government is often called 'centralised government'. He rewarded his supporters with land but did not give them so much that they could challenge him (as you can read below). William also consulted his earls about important issues so that they felt he respected them. For example, before he ordered the survey that led to Domesday Book (see pages 92–93) he had 'deep speech' with his earls, lords and bishops.

William kept the majority of the land in the country for himself. The king's land was known as the royal demesne – demesne comes from a Latin word meaning 'lord'. The royal demesne played a vital part in building William's power. Kings who were not wealthy and did not show off their wealth looked vulnerable to attack and rebellion. This income from his demesne paid for William's castles, his servants and all the needs of his family, but also allowed William to show himself off as a rich, magnificent and unchallengeable ruler. For example, he held splendid, crown-wearing ceremonies at court three times a year (at Christmas, Easter and Whit), designed to show off his power and magnificence.

Another reason why William was powerful was that he was physically at the centre of decision-making – government did not take place in buildings separate from the king. As the diagram below shows, the king was the centre of decision-making and power.

ROYAL LUXURY

William showed off his power through the luxury of his clothes and buildings. One chronicler wrote 'kings are like gods to their subjects. People never weary of looking at them. Crowds rush to gaze at them!' You can find examples on pages 100–101.

1 How did William keep his lords' loyalty?

2 How did William show off his power and why was this important?

3 Why was the royal demesne so important?

4 Explain why the king was always physically at the centre of government and decisions taken.

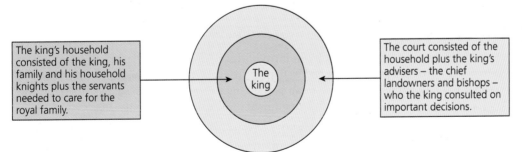

The king's household consisted of the king, his family and his household knights plus the servants needed to care for the royal family.

The king

The court consisted of the household plus the king's advisers – the chief landowners and bishops – who the king consulted on important decisions.

◀ The household and court were not physical buildings. They were groups of people. For example, the court was wherever the members of the court were, which could be in Winchester, London or wherever the king chose to be. The household and court moved with him.

Regents

We could easily assume that once William became King of England he spent all or most of his time in England. However, William was still Duke of Normandy and just as determined to defend Normandy as England. Rebellions forced him to be in England much of the time between 1066 and 1072, but dangers to Normandy meant that between 1072 and his death in 1087, William spent 80 per cent of his time in Normandy.

So, while William was in Normandy, who was in control in England? William's answer was to appoint one of his most trusted supporters as regent with the same powers that William had. On different occasions he gave this power to his half-brother, Odo of Bayeux, to his long-standing friend, William fitzOsbern, Earl of Chester, and to Lanfranc, his trusted Archbishop of Canterbury. This system worked successfully which shows two things: that William chose his regents wisely, and that he had built up a strong and effective system of government for them to use.

5 Why were regents needed?

6 What can we learn from the success of the regents?

The power of the earls

William was generous to his supporters, especially to the great Norman lords who had brought many men to fight at Hastings. He gave them the title of 'earl' and large quantities of English land – just ten of them together held around a quarter of the land in England. In today's language they were multi-millionaires many times over.

However, William took care not to make his earls too powerful. He did not want their power to rival his, as had happened during Edward the Confessor's reign. The new earldoms he created were smaller and less wealthy than the huge Saxon earldoms of Wessex, Mercia and Northumbria.

7 'William was foolishly generous to his supporters.' Would you agree? If not explain why and how you would describe the rewards he gave his supporters?

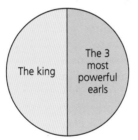

Edward the Confessor's reign

The three English most powerful earls were, together, as rich as the king.

William's reign

The ten most powerful Normans did not, together, have as much wealth as the king. In fact, the king held twice as much land as everyone else put together.

The role of the sheriffs

In a period when horses were the fastest form of travel, it was difficult for kings to deal quickly with problems that happened well away from their base in the south-east. Anglo-Saxon kings had appointed a shire-reeve as the king's chief official in each county and the king sent him instructions in written documents called 'writs' (see page 14).

This system was well established and William continued to use it although the term 'shire-reeve' developed into sheriff. It was particularly important that the king's own lands in each county – the royal demesne – were run efficiently. The sheriffs were expected to:

- follow the instructions received in writs
- collect taxes and fines due to the king
- carry out justice in the king's courts, punishing criminals to show the king's power
- raise soldiers for the royal army whenever they were needed.

William hoped to continue using Englishmen as sheriffs, another example of him not wanting to alienate the English and push them into rebellion. However, after the rebellions of 1067–71 he replaced English sheriffs with Normans. (One of the English sheriffs was Tofi in Somerset. I wonder if he came to a 'sticky' end?) He also appointed more powerful individuals with more land (Anglo-Saxon sheriffs had often been second-rank landowners) so that they were no longer playing second-fiddle to the earls. For the English, these Norman sheriffs with their increased power were another symbol of Norman control of England.

8 What work did sheriffs do?

9 How were Norman sheriffs more powerful than their Anglo-Saxon predecessors?

The forest and forest laws

WHAT WAS A FOREST?

NOT THIS!

A forest was *not* an area with a lot of trees! A forest was any area of land the king said was to be used chiefly for hunting. It could have trees, but it could also be open farmland. More importantly these 'forests' had their own legal system. They were called 'forests' because the word 'forest' comes from the Latin word 'foris' which means 'outside the normal legal system'.

The new Norman forests were used for hunting, an enjoyable pastime for the wealthy but also excellent training for war, requiring high-quality riding skills and mastery of the bow and arrow. The Normans' use of forests was deeply hated by the English. Anglo-Saxon kings had hunted, but they had not set huge areas of land aside for hunting as William did. When he created the New Forest in Hampshire, 2,000 people were moved and 12 villages destroyed to make hunting easier. It had not been good farmland but it was a huge disruption to normal life.

However, it was the new Forest Laws that caused most hatred. Many people still lived and farmed in the forests, but William set up a different legal system for the forests with much harsher laws. Anyone caught hunting in the forest faced blinding or execution. No one was even allowed to own a bow. Cutting down trees and collecting wood to repair homes or for fuel were illegal. These laws were administered by specially appointed forest officials who held their own courts to punish offenders. Fines were high and the money went straight to the king's treasury, helping make William wealthier. Another advantage for William was that when rebels hid in the new forest areas his own officials could hunt them down.

The establishment of huge areas as forest and the new system of Forest Laws shows just how powerful William was. This was hated by the English but they were powerless to stop him doing what he wanted.

10 Why were forests hated by the English?
11 What do the forests tell us about William's power?

The significance of Domesday Book

In 1085 William again faced a threat to his hold on England. A Danish invasion seemed imminent and William had to raise an army and keep it supplied until the threat was over. This threat may explain why William ordered the Domesday Survey at Christmas 1085. The Anglo-Saxon Chronicle described what happened:

> The King sent his men all over England, into every shire and had them find out how much land the king, the bishops and the lords had in each county and how much that land was worth. So very detailed was this investigation that there was no land, no ox, no cow, no sheep nor one pig left out (I am ashamed to write this but he was not ashamed to do it), and all these records were brought to him.

We don't definitely know why William ordered the survey but the invasion threat may have led William to sort out who had each area of land and what taxes each man should pay. Since 1066 he had given lands to his lords and bishops in so many bits and pieces that nobody knew in detail who had which lands. With accurate information William could raise taxes and feed his army more efficiently.

Collecting the information for the Domesday Survey from nearly the whole country was a huge task but took less than a year, largely because the Normans used the very efficient Anglo-Saxon administrative system. The results were written up in what became known as Domesday Book. It may have been left unfinished because William died.

The Survey gives us a great deal of information about individual villages but it also tells us the following:

- William was an exceedingly powerful king to have such a detailed survey carried out with great accuracy. Everyone must have feared the consequences if they lied to the royal commissioners about the value of land.
- William was extremely wealthy. It details exactly which lands everyone owned and how much they were worth so we can compare the wealth of the king and his lords (see page 90).
- William and his successors now had the power to tax people effectively because they knew how much income everyone had. It was impossible to claim you could not afford the king's taxes and be believed.

◀ The entry in Domesday Book for Kennett in Cambridgeshire. This is the final version after all the information has been collected, then edited down to the essentials. An earlier version recorded 8 cattle, 480 sheep, 10 pigs and 4 horses in Kennett. It also gave the names of the local men who gave evidence to William's commissioners. (A hide was measurement of land.) The box underneath is a translation into modern English.

12 What reasons may explain why the Domesday Survey was carried out?

13 Why was the Anglo-Saxon Chronicle so hostile to the survey?

14 What does the survey tell us about William's power?

KENNETT was taxed in the time of *King Edward* on three and a half hides of land. It is still taxed on three and a half hides of land. It is held by **William de Warenne**. There are five ploughs on the lord's land and twelve villagers have another five ploughs. There are twelve slaves, a mill, a meadow and pasture for all the village animals. In all it is worth twelve pounds. When William received it was worth nine pounds. In the time of *King Edward* it was held by *Tochil*, a lord of *King Edward* and it was worth twelve pounds.

Visible learning

Jogging your memory

You will have a lot to remember for your exam so using your memory techniques will help you. How will you remember the changes in government? Perhaps the FIVE FREDS will help you – but first you have to work out what they mean! Think about the topics in this chapter.

GRENTEBRSCIRE

TRE – In the time of King Edward

Name of county – Cambridgeshire

Lands are recorded under the names of each landholder. A red heading identifies a new section, in this case the lands of Robert Gernon

The signs that look like the number 7 means 'and'

▲ A page of entries in the Domesday Book for the county of Cambridgeshire. The entry for Kennett on page 92 can be seen halfway down the left column.

6.6 Communicating your answers

This chapter has had one overall question: 'How did William's needs change England?' Whenever you are asked to explain why changes happened – or why there were continuities – it is vital to think about what people or individuals at the time needed. Changes very rarely happen 'out of the blue' – they happen because someone, in this case King William, has a need or problem and takes actions to solve that problem.

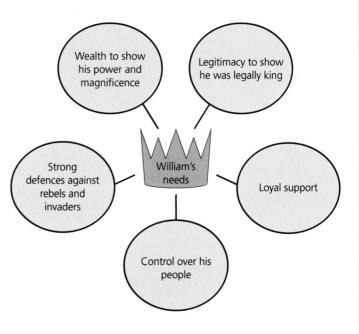

After 1066 William needed the things you can see in the diagram on the right. At first he hoped the English would not rebel and he tried not to push them into rebellion. This was why he did not immediately take land away from all the English landholders. However, once rebellions began and were clearly dangerous, his needs drove his actions – at first he built castles and punished people with the savage destruction of property and animals and of the rebels themselves. As time went on he made other changes, but all were the results of the needs in the diagram. He did not do this simply because he was Norman and the people were English. He did it because he needed to establish control and show everyone he was now king.

Practice questions

The question 'How did William's needs change England?' has been a good question for linking all the topics in this chapter together and it is an important question for understanding the Norman Conquest. However, it is not the style of question you will have to answer in your exam. Therefore, we are not asking you to write an answer to that question. Instead you and your teacher will choose a question or questions from this box or similar questions to tackle. When answering them, use the guidelines on pages 114–123 to produce the best possible answers.

1 Describe two features of:
   a) feudalism
   b) Lanfranc's reforms of the English Church
   c) the Forest Laws
   d) Domesday Book.
2 Explain why Lanfranc made changes to the Church in England.
3 Explain why changes took place in Anglo-Saxon society and economy after 1066.
4 'The main consequence of changes in government after 1066 was that the king had more power than his Anglo-Saxon predecessors.' How far do you agree? Explain your answer.
5 'The main consequence of religious reforms was that English cathedrals were all rebuilt.' How far do you agree? Explain your answer.

Revisiting your Word Wall

When answering any exam questions on this chapter, at least some of the words below will be useful to you. Make sure you know what each one means and how to use them all effectively.

feudalism   feudal hierarchy   tenants-in-chief   landholding   homage

knight service   labour service   forfeiture   Normanisation   centralisation   sheriff

trial by combat   regents   demesne   Forest Law   Domesday Book

7 William I, his sons and the Norman aristocracy

This chapter continues to explore the similarities and differences between Anglo-Saxon and Norman England. Before 1066 there had been conflicts between Anglo-Saxon nobles (between Harold Godwinson and his brother Tostig, for example) and crises over who should be the next king. Therefore the question we shall be exploring in this chapter is:

Did conflicts and crises continue after 1066 or did William, his family and the Norman aristocracy work together peacefully?

We shall answer this question by investigating four topics:

1 The Norman aristocracy – their culture and language

2 The career of Odo, Bishop of Bayeux and Earl of Kent

3 Robert of Normandy, King William's eldest son

4 The events after King William's death

DECISION TIME

The three decisions below introduce some of the major events in this chapter.

1 For each decision choose one of the options provided. Make a note of your choice as you will find out what happened later in the chapter.

2 What do the events described in the decisions suggest about rivalry and conflicts among the Normans after 1066?

DECISION 1

It is 1079. King William's eldest son, Robert, has rebelled against his father in Normandy. William and his army are now attacking Robert's castle at Gerberoi. Do you think Robert should:

1 make peace with his father, King William? This would show loyalty to his father and stop William's enemies in France and Scotland taking advantage of this trouble.

2 open the castle gates and ride out to fight William? Robert is an adult but William often insults him and refuses to let him govern Normandy.

DECISION 2

It is 1082. King William's half-brother, Bishop Odo, is planning a military expedition to Italy. Odo has often been a great support for William, but has also caused trouble. William has ordered him not to go to Italy because his knights may be needed to defend England. However, Odo is continuing with his plans. He may be planning to use his army to make himself Pope. Do you think that William should:

1 ignore Odo and let him leave for Italy? This will get his trouble-making brother out of the way.

2 imprison his brother? This will prove to Odo and everyone else that William is still in charge and powerful. After Robert's rebellion it is important for William to demonstrate his power.

DECISION 3

It is 1088. William the Conqueror has died. His eldest son, Robert, rules Normandy but his second son, William Rufus, is King of England. This creates a problem for nobles with land in both Normandy and England. Which brother should they obey if war breaks out between them?

A rebellion is being planned against William Rufus. The aim is to make Robert of Normandy, King of England. As a Norman nobleman should you:

1 fight for Robert in the rebellion against William Rufus? If it succeeds Robert will become King of England and unite Normandy and England again. This will solve the problem of which ruler to obey.

2 fight for William Rufus? He acted quickly to take the English crown. He may turn out to be a much harsher ruler than Robert but kings need to be harsh.

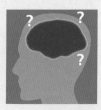

7.1 The Norman aristocracy

This illustration helps you visualise the lives of the Norman aristocracy. They were the great lords who took control of land all over England. They kept their land in Normandy and travelled regularly between the two countries. The information around the illustration explains the culture of these aristocrats – 'culture' means how they thought, behaved and what was important to them.

What do we call them?
Aristocrats, nobles, lords, barons – these are all words for the same people, the most powerful and wealthy men who held the most land.

This is the hall in a lord's castle in Normandy. As time went by, lords built stone halls and castles like this in England to show off their wealth, their power and status. The lord, his family and their guests sit at the top table. They were served first and ate the best food.

Chess and dice were common games. Both led to a lot of gambling.

Nobles were expected to be generous to the knights who fought for them. Gifts of land, warhorses or hunting dogs showed that a nobleman was a good man to follow because he was honourable and living as a nobleman should.

The children of noblemen were taught good manners, how to eat politely and the importance of being clean. Hands and faces were washed regularly.

Jesters and **minstrels** sang and played music as entertainment. Two jesters are mentioned in Domesday Book because they were given lands by their lords.

THE NORMAN ARISTOCRACY ?

1. Which personal qualities were most important to the aristocracy?

2. Which details in the illustration show the high standard of living of the Norman lords? Explain your choices.

3. Why did the nobles continue to speak French when they lived in England?

4. How did nobles spend their time when not fighting for the king?

5. Why was learning to ride so important?

7.2 The significance of Odo, Bishop of Bayeux

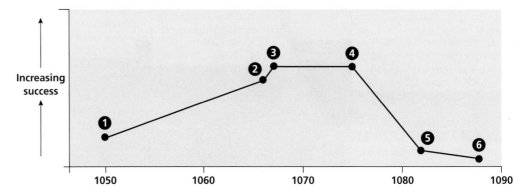

Increasing success

▲ The highs and lows of the career of Bishop Odo.

ODO OF BAYEUX ❓

1 The graph above summarises the high and low points in Odo's career. Read pages 98 and 99 and identify each of points 1–6.

2 What evidence from pages 98–99 supports each of these statements?
   a) William trusted Odo to maintain Norman control of England.
   b) Norman rulers were often cruel and ruthless to the English.
   c) Odo was proud of his role in the Norman Conquest of England.
   d) William was ruthless in his treatment of anyone who opposed or disobeyed him.

3 Odo was a significant person in the history of the Norman Conquest because …

   How would you complete this paragraph to explain what Odo's career reveals about the events and impact of the Norman Conquest?

Visible learning

Using knowledge effectively to justify conclusions

It is always easy to make an assertion about a person or event, such as 'Odo played a significant part in the Norman Conquest', but we must always provide evidence to justify such statements. This is why it is important you are knowledgeable – that you have detailed and accurate knowledge in your mind to use as evidence. Do not just put down any evidence to support your statement but try to choose the **best** evidence that best **proves** your point. And finally remember to use connectives to link the evidence to your statements such as:

- This shows that …
- This tells us that …
- The evidence that best supports this is …

Odo's career until 1066

Odo was Duke William's half-brother. They had the same mother, Herleva, but different fathers. Odo was born in the early 1030s but we do not know much about his childhood or youth. We do know that Duke William appointed Odo as Bishop of Bayeux before he was twenty years old. Odo was not chosen because he was deeply religious but because William wanted one of his close relatives as the Bishop of Bayeux, one of the most important towns in Normandy.

Odo did work hard as bishop, but he was always more interested in military and political matters than in the Church. One source says that he organised and paid for 100 ships for the invasion of England in 1066. By then Odo was in his early thirties, a mature man and an experienced and effective leader.

▲ Historians believe that it was Odo who arranged and paid for the Bayeux Tapestry to be made. It was probably embroidered in England, but the story in the Tapestry followed Odo's orders. In this section of the Tapestry, Odo (on the left) is shown advising William before the Battle of Hastings. Odo appears to be doing the talking while William and their other brother, Robert of Mortain, listen to his wisdom.

▲ Odo, holding a club, is shown urging forward the soldiers at the Battle of Hastings. Odo holds a club, not a sword, because, as a churchman, he was not allowed to shed blood. Crushing skulls, however, seems to be acceptable!

Odo's career after the Conquest

After 1066 Odo played a leading part in the Conquest and governing of England. William's trust in his brother was shown in a number of ways:

1 William gave Odo a huge amount of land worth £3,000 a year. Only a handful of men had land worth £750 a year, the equivalent of a multi-millionaire today. Only William had more land in England than Odo.

2 Odo was appointed Earl of Kent in 1067. This showed William's trust because Kent, in the south-east of England, was a vital area that needed defending against rebellions and invasion. In 1067 Odo had to defend Kent against attack by William's former ally, Eustace, Count of Boulogne.

3 William made Odo his regent in England on several occasions when he returned to Normandy. As regent, Odo took over William's powers. Clearly William believed his brother was a reliable and capable deputy, although Odo often shared the powers of regent with others such as Lanfranc, Archbishop of Canterbury.

4 In 1075 (as you saw on page 73), Odo led the king's army to defeat the Earl of Norfolk and end the Revolt of the Earls. In 1080 Odo was put in charge of the army that devastated Northumbria as punishment for the murder of the new Norman bishop of Durham.

Odo certainly showed himself just as harsh as William in his treatment of the English. He was hated by them. His treatment of the people of Kent provoked rebellion there in 1067 and he was described as a 'ravening wolf' by one chronicler. Orderic Vitalis, who was half-Saxon, half-Norman, described Odo as a tyrant, a ruler who ignored fairness and the law in order to seize land from its owners.

Imprisonment and rebellion

Odo's wish for more power eventually led to conflict with William, as you saw in the decision-making activity on page 95. In 1082 Odo planned a military expedition to Italy. He may have hoped to be made Pope and planned to use force to 'persuade' others to support him. William ordered Odo to abandon the plan, partly because Odo's soldiers might be needed to defend England. However, Odo carried on until William, tired of his brother's ambition, had Odo arrested and imprisoned in Rouen in Normandy. William kept Odo in prison for the rest of his reign.

Odo was released by the dying William but probably only because nobles pleaded for his freedom. William did not forgive easily! Odo then continued to cause problems for William Rufus, the new King of England. Odo was the central figure in a rebellion against Rufus, as you will read on pages 104–106. Odo's plans failed and Rufus banished and disinherited Odo, who then set off on **Crusade**. He died on the way to Jerusalem in 1097.

7.3 William I and his family

One man dominates the story of the Norman Conquest – William the Conqueror. What kind of man was he? What did he look like? What qualities made him so successful?

We know little about William's appearance. There are no pictures of William which look lifelike, so we have to rely on written descriptions such as this, by William of Jumieges, a monk in Normandy:

> He was great in body and strong, tall in stature but not ungainly. He was temperate in eating and drinking … If his voice was harsh, what he said was always suited to the occasion.

One piece of evidence suggests he was five feet and ten inches tall, but even this evidence is questionable. When William's tomb was ransacked in 1562 his skeleton disappeared. In 1642, when a new monument was built, a priest produced a thigh bone that he claimed was William's. If the thigh bone is William's, its length suggests he was about five feet and ten inches tall but no-one knows if it is really William's.

This diagram summarises the main things we know about William's appearance from written sources:

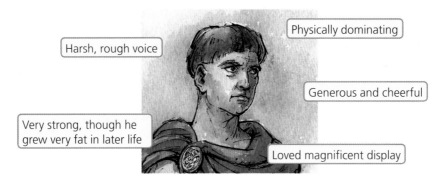

Harsh, rough voice

Physically dominating

Generous and cheerful

Very strong, though he grew very fat in later life

Loved magnificent display

WILLIAM, HIS CHARACTER AND QUALITIES

1 The blue boxes 1–7 below describe William's qualities. The yellow boxes A–K provide evidence of those qualities. Match up the evidence with the qualities. You can use more than one yellow box to support a blue box.

2 Which qualities do you think made him a successful soldier and king?

1 Loved hunting

2 Ruthless, brutal and cruel

3 Politically intelligent

4 Highly energetic

5 Religious

6 Brave and inspiring

7 Magnificent appearance

A He travelled from Normandy to England many times.

B He ordered the Harrying of the North after the rebellions of 1069.

C He founded Battle Abbey and gave a great deal of money and land to the Church.

D He kept Wulfnoth, Harold's last surviving brother, as a hostage from 1051 until 1087.

E His leadership at the Battle of Hastings.

F He did not take land from Anglo-Saxon landowners immediately after 1066, because he feared this would lead to rebellion.

G The New Forest was created for hunting and anyone killing the king's deer was savagely punished.

H He was still leading a military campaign in the month before he died, aged 60.

I He ordered his own half-brother, Odo, to be imprisoned.

J One day William appeared for dinner wearing so much dazzling jewellery and gold cloth that an observer remarked 'Behold, I see God!'

K William tried to learn English so he could understand court cases without an interpreter but he never succeeded.

QUEEN MATILDA

Matilda married William around 1050. She was the daughter of the Count of Flanders, another important ruler in France. It seems that William and Matilda had a happy marriage and there is no evidence that he was unfaithful to her. She was close to their children, especially Robert. Matilda acted as regent (William's deputy) in Normandy while he was in England in 1066 and on other occasions. She died in 1083, four years before William.

OTHER CHILDREN

William and Matilda had six children in addition to the three sons shown below. One son, Richard, was killed hunting. It would be easy to leave their five daughters out of this book as you do not need to know about them for your exam – and they did not rebel against William or fight each other, like their brothers! However, they were real people, just like their brothers. Their names were Adelida, Cecilia, Matilda, Constance and Adela. Adela's son, Stephen, became King of England in 1135.

ROBERT OF NORMANDY, C.1053–1134

Robert was nicknamed Curthose, which meant 'Short Boots'. Less complimentary was another nickname – 'Fat Legs'. He was round-faced, talkative and cheerful, short and stout – which is a polite way of saying 'getting fat'. Despite this, Robert was a great soldier when he was young, even wounding his father in battle when he rebelled. Later he became a brave and famous Crusader. When he came back from Crusade he had to fight his brother Henry for control of Normandy – but lost. Henry kept Robert in a comfortable prison in Cardiff castle for the rest of his life, while Henry ruled both Normandy and England.

WILLIAM RUFUS, C.1060–1100, KING OF ENGLAND, 1087–1100

William is known as Rufus to avoid mixing him up with his father. The name was probably not used in his lifetime, but was used soon afterwards. It comes from his red complexion and red hair which went blond as he grew older. He was also short and grew fat though, like his father, he was a great soldier, energetic and intelligent. As King of England after 1087 he twice invaded Normandy to try to take it from his brother Robert. He was killed in a hunting accident in the New Forest in 1100.

Like his father, Rufus knew that it was important to look wealthy and powerful. He also enjoyed wearing expensive clothes. The chronicler, William of Malmesbury, wrote that one morning Rufus lost his temper when his servant gave him a pair of shoes to wear that had been cheap to buy. 'Since when has a king worn such cheap shoes,' stormed Rufus, 'get me some that cost at least twice as much.'

HENRY, 1069–1135, KING OF ENGLAND, 1100–1135

Henry was the youngest son but succeeded in reuniting England and Normandy after he became King in 1100. Henry beat his brother Robert in battle and held him prisoner for the rest of his life. Henry became fat late in life very like his father and was short like his brothers. He was also completely ruthless and at times very cruel, but highly successful as king.

WILLIAM'S FAMILY

?

1 Draw a family tree or diagram showing King William's family.
2 What did the brothers have in common physically?
3 Why was this family more likely to play Monopoly than Happy Families?

Visible learning

Family trees

It is easy to be confused by historical families. The names can be hard to remember even before you try to work out who is related to who! You will find it easier to sort out and remember family connections if you draw your own family trees or plans and annotate them with your own explanations. This is much more effective than simply looking at a family tree in a book.

7.4 William, Robert and revolt in Normandy, 1077–80

Robert of Normandy, William's eldest son, was aged about 16 in 1066 when William became King of England. It seemed that William trusted Robert because he made Robert the heir to Normandy when he set off to invade England. However, by the 1070s, the sources suggest that William thought Robert was spoiled and sometimes foolish. When William was in England he trusted Queen Matilda and his nobles to rule Normandy, not Robert.

At the same time Robert became impatient to rule lands for himself. According to the chronicler Orderic Vitalis, Robert told William:

> I am not prepared to be your servant forever. I want to have land of my own so I can reward my followers properly. I ask you to let me rule Normandy just as you rule England.

Robert knew how important it was for him as a nobleman to have the wealth to reward his supporters and so show how honourable he was. If William did not give him the money to do this, it shamed him in the eyes of others.

William refused to give Normandy to Robert. According to William of Malmesbury, a historian writing in the early 1100s, William drove Robert away 'with jeers in that terrific voice', humiliating him in front of the nobles.

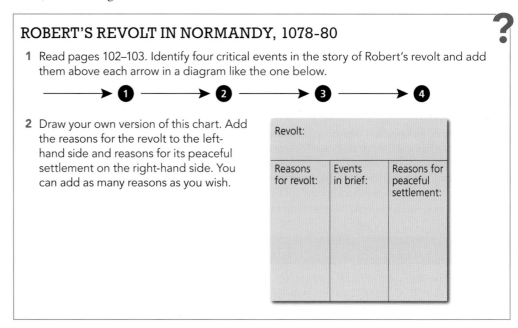

ROBERT'S REVOLT IN NORMANDY, 1078-80 ❓

1 Read pages 102–103. Identify four critical events in the story of Robert's revolt and add them above each arrow in a diagram like the one below.

→ ❶ → ❷ → ❸ → ❹

2 Draw your own version of this chart. Add the reasons for the revolt to the left-hand side and reasons for its peaceful settlement on the right-hand side. You can add as many reasons as you wish.

Revolt:

Reasons for revolt:	Events in brief:	Reasons for peaceful settlement:

The beginnings of the revolt

Robert's anger boiled over early in 1078 when he was about 28. He was angry as William refused to let him take over Normandy. Worse, William now spent most of the time in Normandy and little time in England, so there was even less chance of Robert being given the chance to prove himself in Normandy.

The spark that started his revolt was a brawl with his younger brothers, William Rufus, aged 18, and Henry, who was about 10. William and Henry may have been angry at Robert's attempts to gain power. Whatever the reason, they decided to have fun by standing in the gallery of a house and urinating down on to the heads of Robert and his friends in the hall below. Robert raced upstairs to deal with them and this turned into a brawl. King William was summoned to stop his sons fighting.

Next morning Robert fled with a group of followers and tried to take control of William's castle at Rouen. They failed, but their revolt had begun. Robert had the support of a large number of young knights, so his revolt was certainly dangerous to William.

Despite the danger William continued to insult his son. He commented sarcastically that 'Little Robert Short Boots' wanted to make himself a hero. William does seem to have underestimated Robert, who was undoubtedly a good soldier.

This split in King William's family was good news for his enemies. The rulers of France and Flanders took advantage. They gave Robert knights and the castle at Gerberoi, knowing this would make it harder for William to defeat his son. They were right. William was about to be humiliated.

Robert's decision – Gerberoi, 1079

Robert and his men carried out raids in Normandy, angering William. He retaliated by marching an army to Gerberoi and besieging Robert in the castle. Robert now faced the decision you tackled on page 95. Should he give in or fight against his own father? He decided to fight – and he won. Robert and his men surged out of the castle and attacked William's army. Robert himself wounded William in the arm. Ironically, William had to be rescued by an Englishman in his army, Toki of Wallingford. William Rufus, fighting for his father, was also wounded.

King William's defeat at Gerberoi made Robert look a great success. It also made William look 'over the hill', a ruler well past his peak. Worse, he found out that Queen Matilda had been sending Robert money while he'd been in revolt. She could not bear her family being at war with each other. Then the King of Scots decided that this was a good time to invade the north of England.

William's decision – war or peace?

The revolt was not just Robert against his father, William. Robert's supporters were the sons of senior Norman nobles, the men who had joined William in his conquest of England. This was a revolt of the younger generation against the older generation.

What should William do? Make peace or continue to fight against his own son? William seems to have been eager to carry on fighting. 'Which of my ancestors ever had to endure such hostility from a child?' he growled. However, everyone else wanted peace, including William's nobles. They were also fighting against their rebellious sons and they did not want to see their sons killed or punished. They wanted peace so that, in time, their sons could inherit and then rule the family lands. Queen Matilda, too, wanted to end the war within her family. 'Her eyes choked with tears', as she begged William to make peace with Robert.

The nobles won the argument. William gave in and agreed to a peace settlement. At Easter 1080, William made peace with Robert and reconfirmed him as his heir in Normandy. To show their new unity, Robert led William's army to defeat the Scottish invaders. During his expedition Robert ordered the building of a new castle in what eventually became one of the largest cities in England – Newcastle.

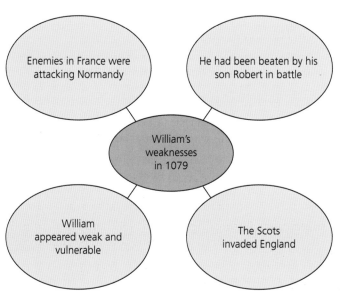

▲ Newcastle castle.

7.5 Death, disputes and revolts, 1087–88

THE SUCCESSION DISPUTE OF 1088 ?

1 Read pages 104–106. Identify four critical events in the story of the revolt led by Odo against William Rufus and add them above each arrow in a diagram like the one below.

→ **1** ——→ **2** ——→ **3** ——→ **4**

2 Draw your own version of the table below then read these pages again more carefully. Complete column 2 of the table, explaining how each reason led to the revolt.

Reasons for the dispute and revolt	How does each reason lead to the revolt?
The relationships between members of William I's family	
William I's decisions about who inherited his land	
Odo's ambitions	
The attitudes and fears of the nobles	
Customs about how land and kingdoms were inherited	

3 Explain why William Rufus made a peaceful settlement with the rebels.

William's death and the succession dispute

By 1086 William I was no longer feared as he had been in earlier years. Robert of Normandy's revolt and success in battle against William had encouraged William's many enemies – the Scots, the French, the Flemings. There were still fears of a major Danish invasion of England. Almost inevitably, it was war that led to William's death in 1087.

This war was a dispute with the French King on the border of Normandy. William attacked and burned the town of Mantes but, riding through the town, his horse reared up and the iron pommel on William's saddle was driven hard into his stomach. This injury did great internal damage and William was carried, dying, to Rouen.

Two of William's sons were at his death-bed – William Rufus and Henry. Robert was not there as he had again gone into exile after more arguments with his father. Although he was dying, William still had one very important decision to make:

Who should succeed him as ruler of Normandy and England?

As usual we cannot be completely certain about what happened and what William wanted because the sources tell different stories. It seems most likely that William did not want to leave Normandy or England to Robert, his eldest son, because he was still angry at his revolt. However, the nobles pleaded with William to keep his earlier promises to make Robert his heir in Normandy. Therefore, William agreed that Robert would be Duke of Normandy. Giving the land to the eldest son fitted in with the usual customs for inheriting land in Normandy.

What about England? William had fought for twenty years to keep England and Normandy together, ruled by one person – himself. Now he did something different. It seems that William could not face leaving all his land to Robert. He wanted Rufus, his favourite son, to be King, even if this meant splitting England and Normandy. Similarly, one of William's greatest noblemen, William fitzOsbern had left his land in Normandy to his eldest son and his English land to his second son.

One chronicle explains what probably happened. William did not leave England directly to Rufus. William said he would leave it to God to decide who would be King because that was how William himself had become King, when God had given him victory in the Battle of Hastings. However, William did give God and Rufus a helping hand! He sent Rufus to England with a letter to Archbishop Lanfranc instructing the archbishop to arrange for William Rufus to be crowned King of England.

Rufus made good use of his headstart. He crossed to England before his father had died. He took control of the royal treasury in Winchester and was soon crowned King with Lanfranc's support.

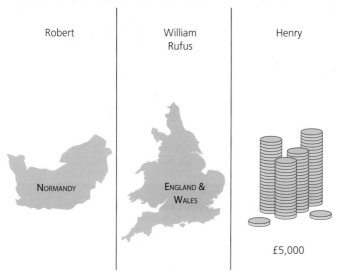

▲ This diagram summarises what each of William's sons inherited.

DID THE ELDEST SON ALWAYS INHERIT HIS FATHER'S LANDS?

Today we expect the eldest child of a king to inherit the crown and land but in the eleventh century the situation was not as clear-cut. Different countries had different customs. Sometimes those customs changed. It was expected that a king would pass on his kingdom to his son, but it need not be his eldest son. So we have to remember that the rules about who inherited land were not so straightforward as they were later in history. In Normandy, the dukes had passed their lands to their eldest sons but none of them had ever been King of England at the same time! Therefore the situation when William died in 1087 was new. In addition, inheritance often depended on the wishes of the king and how he and his heirs got on. A powerful man like William I, even on his death-bed, could make his own rules – and he did.

WHAT HAPPENED TO HENRY, THE YOUNGEST SON?

Henry, then aged 19, was given £5,000 pounds, which does not sound a great deal today but was worth at least 80 times as much in 1087. And in time Henry did exactly what his father had done – he became King of England and united England and Normandy, keeping his brother Robert in prison for the rest of his life!

The nobles' dilemma

The nobles now faced the third decision you looked at on page 95. Many of them held land in both England and Normandy. This had not been a problem while William I had been King, because there was one ruler of both England and Normandy. However, now these nobles had two rulers – they had to do homage to Robert for their lands in Normandy and fight for him if needed. They also had to do homage to William Rufus for their lands in England and fight for him if needed.

What would the nobles do if Robert and his brother Rufus went to war with each other? In theory they were bound by their oaths of loyalty to fight for both men!

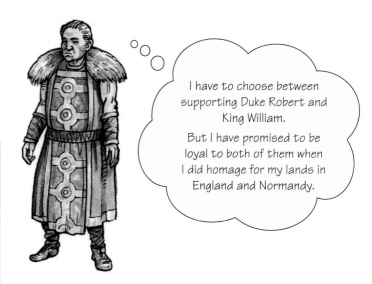

I have to choose between supporting Duke Robert and King William.

But I have promised to be loyal to both of them when I did homage for my lands in England and Normandy.

Bishop Odo came up with an answer. Odo had been freed from prison, reluctantly, by William I on his death-bed. Only his nobles' pleading persuaded William to free his half-brother. Now Odo showed why William had been right to keep him in prison!

Odo said that the Norman nobles should choose between Robert and Rufus and help one of them reunite England and Normandy. Odo suggested they should unite behind Robert and depose Rufus – partly because he knew that Robert would be easier to handle and would be much more likely to listen to the advice of Odo and other nobles. Rufus would be a much stronger, more independent-minded king.

The rebellion of 1088

Rufus must have realised that a rebellion was underway at Easter 1088. When he held his Easter court many nobles stayed away. As the map shows, there were outbreaks of rebellion across the midlands and south, creating a serious threat to Rufus. He had a choice – should he tackle the weaker rebels first or go straight to the dangerous heart of the rebellion? Rufus headed straight for the heart – to Rochester castle where Odo was planning the rebellion.

Rufus' aggression worked. He captured Rochester castle and Odo, bringing a swift end to the rebellion. Rufus was greatly helped by Robert's failure to invade England. Robert had been expected to invade England to aid the rebels, but Robert never left Normandy. Without their figurehead the rebels had nothing to continue fighting for.

What should Rufus do next? Punish the rebels or agree a peaceful settlement? The nobles on the king's side argued for a peaceful settlement just as they had when Robert had rebelled. They knew that harsh punishments might well lead to more rebellions. It was better to treat the rebels generously and win them over to support Rufus.

The succession crisis of 1088 was now over. Bishop Odo was exiled from England for life and, as you have read on page 99, spent the rest of his life in Normandy before dying on the way to the Crusade. William Rufus had established himself as King of England.

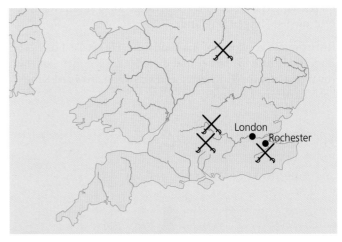

▲ This map shows the main areas of fighting during the revolt. The core of the revolt was at Rochester in Kent.

CHAPTER CONCLUSION

Did conflicts and crises die out after 1066?

At the beginning of this chapter we asked:

Did conflicts and crises continue after 1066 or did William, his family, and the Norman aristocracy work together peacefully?

You have seen plenty of evidence that conflicts continued. Here are three obvious examples:

However, in each case the aristocracy also wanted peace. William I's nobles begged him to make peace with Robert to save their sons from punishment. William II's nobles begged him not to punish the rebels to prevent further rebellion. Nobles even pleaded with William on his death-bed to release Odo from prison.

So conflicts and crises continued but they were not mindless mayhem with everyone fighting to the bitter end. The Norman aristocracy did try to work together, at least in part because they knew that had enough enemies (the English, Scots, French, Danes and more) without destroying each other.

William I v
his brother Odo

William I v
his son Robert

William II v
Odo and Robert

Communicating your answer

Pages 104–106 have investigated the succession dispute of 1087–88. You now have enough information to enable you to answer this question:

Explain why there was a disputed succession to the English throne when William I died.

On pages 118–119 you will find detailed guidance for answering this kind of 'Explain why' question. However, before you look at those pages, think back to your work so far:

1 Use your completed table from page 104 to list the main reasons **why** there was succession dispute.
2 Write a short paragraph summarising your answer to the question, identifying two or three main reasons. This makes sure you have the answer clear in your mind before you begin writing.
3 Plan what sequence you will cover the main reasons in your answer.
4 For each reason. identify one or two pieces of information that justify your statement that a reason led to the dispute. In other words:

Don't just say a reason caused the succession dispute, PROVE it.

To do this, use your connective phrases such as 'this led to' and 'this resulted in'.

Updating your Word Wall

Some of these words will help you with answering the question above but you need to understand all of them – and be ready to use them when you do your exam.

culture	aristocracy	banished	superior	custom	heir
disinherit	bequeath	territories	minstrels	jesters	honour
tyrant	birds of prey	falcons	pommel	Curthose	Rufus	Gerberoi
	assertion	evidence that proves	best evidence		

Practice questions

Use the guidance on pages 114–123 to help you write effective answers to these questions.

1 Describe two features of:
   a) the culture of the Norman aristocracy
   b) the career of Bishop Odo
   c) William I's settlement of the succession in 1087.

2 Explain why Robert of Normandy rebelled against his father in 1077–80.
3 Explain why the rebellion against William Rufus in 1088 was settled.
4 'The main consequence of William I's decisions about the succession was that William Rufus inherited the English crown.' Do you agree? Explain your answer.

Conclusion

How should we remember William of Normandy?

WILLIAM – THE MAN HIMSELF ?

clever	thoughtful	**risk-taking**	religious	**lucky**	exhausted
ruthless	**vicious**	brave	frustrated	inspirational	**angry**
painstaking	magnificent	**meticulous**	energetic	**self-righteous**	well-prepared

1 Choose three of the words from the wall above or choose other words of your own that you think best describe William as you have seen him in Key Topic 3. For each word explain your choice. You could refer to one or more of the aspects of William's life shown below.

William's work with Lanfranc to reform the Church

William's reforms of landholding, the law and government

William's anxiety about Danish attacks and the compilation of Domesday Book

William's responses to the rebellions by his son Robert

William's attitudes to who would be his successors in Normandy and England

WILLIAM'S IMPACT ON ENGLAND ?

On page 9, very near the beginning of this course, we introduced an activity that sums up William's impact on England. The activity uses this set of scales to weigh up William's impact.

A great king who made important and beneficial changes to life in England

A ruthless and cruel king whose reign caused great hardship for the people

Evidence or events that lead to other conclusions

You tackled this activity at the end of Key Topic 2 (page 76), compiling evidence of the impact of William's methods of dealing with rebellions and opposition. Now it's time to repeat that activity using the evidence in Key Topic 3, which has examined William's longer-term policies and their effects on England.

Think back over Chapters 6 and 7 in Key Topic 3. Which events, policies or changes to life in England would you place on the set of scales or on the sheet alongside?

Visible learning: Revise and remember

Technique 1: Retelling the stories

Retell the story of one of the events in the blue boxes from the perspective of one of the people listed below. You could choose to tell each one from William's viewpoint and then again from the view of someone else.

- King William I
- Robert of Normandy
- William Rufus
- Odo
- Queen Matilda
- A Norman nobleman
- An English villager
- Lanfranc

The work of Archbishop Lanfranc	Life in English villages after 1066	The introduction of the Forest Laws	The career of Bishop Odo
The compiling of Domesday Book	The revolt of Robert of Normandy	The disputed succession after William I's death	

Technique 2: Using mnemonics to 'make it stick'

Six Nuns Playing Marbles

You have met mnemonics before, including the FREDS on page 92. Mnemonics can be a really powerful way of helping information stick to your brain because they create a memorable image in your mind – even if it's very hard to remember how to spell mnemonic!

1   The question is – what does this image and the letters SNPM help you remember? The answer is in Chapter 6 and it's something to do with religion!

2   Create two more mnemonics to help you remember other information from Key Topic 3.

Technique 3: Test yourself

You need to work at making your knowledge stick in your brain! The more you recap what you have learned and identify **what you're not sure about**, the more chance you have of success. Answer these questions, identify what you don't know and keep repeating this.

1 What was knight service?	2 Name the three main earldoms in Anglo-Saxon England.	3 Why was it important for Norman lords to be generous to their followers?	4 List three problems in the Church which Lanfranc wanted to reform.
5 Which castle was at the centre of the revolt against William Rufus in 1088?	6 What were men who held land *directly* from the king called?	7 List William's three sons who were alive in 1087 – in order of age!	8 What was the Murdrum fine?
9 List in order of hierarchy the groups of people in Anglo-Saxon society.	10 Who or what was Gerberoi?	11 Name two people who acted as William's regent in England.	12 In which year did William I die?

Chapter 8 Conclusions

William I is one of the most famous kings in English history. If you have one of those rulers that list kings and queens on one side he is usually at the beginning of the list, as if there had been no kings worth including before 1066. This means that William is better known than other highly significant kings such as Alfred the Great (870–99), Alfred's son Edward, and grandson Athelstan – the men who created the nation of England by rebuilding and uniting it during and after the Viking invasions. William is often thought of as an English king but he spoke no English and spent little time in England, at most only 20 per cent of his time in the last 15 years of his reign.

◄ This statue is in the centre of Falaise, William's birthplace in Normandy. It shows very clearly how William has been seen in Normandy but does he deserve to be portrayed like this?

HOW SHOULD WE REMEMBER WILLIAM OF NORMANDY?

So how should we remember William? As this is the conclusion this is the time to reach your final verdict on William. You have used the scales before.

1 What evidence would you collect to put on each side of the scales or on the paper alongside them?

2 Read the two views of William opposite. Is there anything in them that you wish to add to the scales?

3 What is your verdict on William? Do you agree with one or other statement on the scales or do you have a different view? Write your own verdict, identifying the most persuasive evidence that supports your viewpoint.

4 Why do you think it is difficult to reach a clear-cut verdict on William that everyone will agree with? Again it will help to refer to the two views opposite.

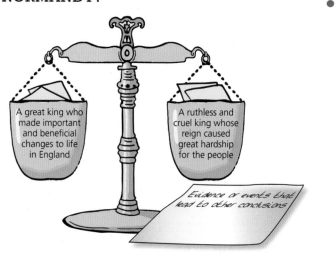

A great king who made important and beneficial changes to life in England

A ruthless and cruel king whose reign caused great hardship for the people

Evidence or events that lead to other conclusions

This verdict on William was written after his death in the late eleventh century or early twelfth century in the Anglo-Saxon Chronicle.

William was a hard and fierce man; no man dared go against his will. He put earls in chains, deposed bishops from their bishoprics and put thegns in prison. He did not even spare his own brother, Odo, a very powerful bishop, an earl in England and master of this land when William was in Normandy. Even Odo was put in prison. Among other things it should not be forgotten that he made peace in this land so that a man laden with gold could travel across the country without being robbed. No man dared kill another, even if he had done much evil to him and if any man lay with a woman against her will he soon lost those limbs he played with.

He reigned over England and controlled and searched it so that he knew what every hide of land was worth and what tax he could collect from it and he had this information set down in his book. Wales was in his power and he had castles built there. He subjected Scotland to his great strength. If he had lived two more years he would have won Ireland with his cunning. Truly in his time men were greatly oppressed and suffered many injuries.

He had castles built and oppressed poor men;

The king was very hard

And took from his people many coins of gold

And many more hundreds of pounds in silver

Into avarice was he fallen

He set many deer free and made laws that whoever

killed a stag or a doe was to be blinded

He loved the stags as if he were their father.

The rich complained and the poor wept

But he was too merciless to care that he was hated.

They had to obey him.

Or they lost their lives and their lands

And their goods and the king's friendship.

May Almighty God show mercy to his soul

And grant him forgiveness for his sins.

Professor David Bates is one of the leading historians writing on William and on both Normandy and England in the eleventh century. These quotations are from the conclusion of his book *William the Conqueror*, published in 1989.

William's importance as a Duke of Normandy is obvious; his personality channelled a Norman and northern French drive towards expansion into successful conquests ... When, however, we ask questions about his importance as a king of the English, then the answers are much more complex, and are likely to be controversial ... it is my opinion that the Conquest represents a dramatic and revolutionary transformation in England's, and Britain's, history. It seems to me undeniable that William's success brought England into closer cultural and political contact with France and that this development had profound consequences for the aristocracy, people and Church ... William's conquest also ended the long-standing relationship between England and Scandinavia and ensured that England would never again be vulnerable to invasion from across the North Sea.

As to changes within England itself, it is impossible to be so certain; there is still fierce controversy [among historians]. My own view is that the initial impact of the Normans was a shattering one, but that in the midst of the slaughter and oppression, William's rule took over and preserved ... a well-developed English system of central and local government ...

I think that the last words can be given to the compassionate Orderic Vitalis. Ultimately he saw William as an extremely successful man, whose success had been gained at enormous cost in terms of innocent human blood ... [Orderic believed that God] would remember, as we always should, the countless, usually silent, victims of a savage and pitiless career.

The Norman Conquest – a personal conclusion

My name is Ian Dawson, one of the writers of this book. I'd like to finish this book with the illustration opposite, which may look unusual. At the top is the American war cemetery above Omaha Beach in Normandy where many soldiers killed in the D-Day landings of 1944 are buried. Below is an artist's drawing of what is obviously a fake cemetery, containing people from the period of the Norman Conquest. What's the idea?

Years ago I had an exceptional group of students who went on two visits to battlefields – to Bosworth where Henry VII killed Richard III in 1485 and to Omaha Beach. At Bosworth everyone did the work I'd set but laughed and joked as usual but at Omaha Beach everyone scattered to be on their own. Nobody said a word. Tears were shed. Why the difference?

To be honest I'm not entirely sure. It's something to do with the distance in time, something to do with the events of the two World Wars being embedded in our consciousness, something to do with whether there are headstones we can read, headstones which give us the names of real people. What I'm trying to show is that the history of the Norman Conquest is, above all, about real individual people. It was a time of huge change and fear. As the chronicler William of Malmesbury wrote several decades later, the Battle of Hastings was 'a fatal day. Now we are ruled by foreigners and strangers'. If we had been born a thousand years ago, it would have been us.

What happened to …?

You know what happened to many of the people you have read about in this book but here are some endings, happy or otherwise!

Morcar was imprisoned for life. No one knows when he died.

Wulfnoth was a younger brother of King Harold. He was sent to Normandy in 1051 as a hostage. Harold went to Normandy to free him but failed. Wulfnoth died around 1094 after spending almost his whole life as a prisoner, albeit living in some comfort.

Edgar Aethling lived to be 75. He had rebelled against William, was pardoned and lived peacefully in England until 1085, travelled to Italy and owned land there, returned to help Robert of Normandy fight against William Rufus, led an Anglo-Norman army to fight in Scotland, went on the First Crusade and much more. A remarkable life.

Reinfred, a Norman soldier, visited Whitby in Yorkshire, saw the damaged abbey and decided to become a monk himself. He went to live at Evesham Abbey and took his vows as a monk, then returned to Whitby to help refound the monastery. Perhaps he was paying a debt for his part in the Harrying?

Ralph of Norfolk and his wife Emma escaped to France after the revolt of 1075 and spent the next twenty years in France. Then they joined the First Crusade and travelled with the army led by Robert of Normandy. They died on Crusade around 1098 before reaching Jerusalem.

Edith, wife of Edward the Confessor, retained most of her land after 1066 and lived comfortably until her death in 1075.

King Harold's children: we know very little about the lives of Harold's six (possibly more) children. They fled abroad, to Denmark and Norway where they had plenty of relatives (see page 10). One daughter, Gytha, went to Denmark, then married a Russian, Prince Vladimir of Kiev. Thanks to Gytha, some of King Harold's descendants ruled parts of Russia.

Introducing the exam

Simply knowing a lot of content is not enough to achieve a good grade in your GCSE history exam. You need to know how to write effective answers to the questions. Pages 114–123 give you an insight into the exam and provide guidance on how to approach the different questions.

This page introduces the structure of Section B (the British depth study) of your Paper 2 exam. The guidance opposite helps you to approach your exam with confidence.

Paper 2 is divided into two sections. Section A covers the **period study**. Section B covers the British **depth study**, where you will select: **Option B1: Anglo-Saxon and Norman England, c1060–88**

Paper 2: Period study and British depth study

(1) **Time allowed: 1 hour 45 minutes**

There are two sections in this question paper. Answer all questions from Section A and EITHER Question 4 or Question 5 in Section B.

The total mark for this paper is 64.

(2) The marks for each question are shown in brackets.

SECTION B: The British depth study

Option B1: Anglo-Saxon and Norman England, c1060–88

(3) Answer Question 4(a), 4(b) and EITHER 4(c)(i) or 4(c)(ii).

(4) 4. **(a)** Describe **two** features of Anglo-Saxon society. (4 marks)

Feature 1:
Feature 2:

(5) **(b)** Explain why there was a disputed succession to the English throne when Edward the Confessor died. (12 marks)

(6)
> You may use the following in your answer:
> - the wealth of Anglo-Saxon England
> - Harold Godwinson.
>
> You **must** also use information of your own.

(7) Answer EITHER (c)(i) OR(c)(ii).

EITHER

(8) **(c)(i)** 'The main reason William I was able to keep control of England in the years 1066–75 was because of his ferocious punishments of rebels.' How far do you agree? Explain your answer. (16 marks)

> You may use the following in your answer:
> - changes in land ownership
> - motte and bailey castles.
>
> You **must** also use information of your own.

OR

(c)(ii) 'The main consequence of the appointment of Lanfranc as Archbishop of Canterbury in 1070 was an increase in cathedral building.' How far do you agree? Explain your answer. (16 marks)

> You may use the following in your answer:
> - Archbishop Stigand
> - monasteries.
>
> You **must** also use information of your own.

Planning for success

1 TIMING

It is important to time yourself carefully. One hour and 45 minutes sounds a long time, but it goes very quickly! Section A (period study) and Section B (British depth study) are worth the same amount of marks. You should aim to spend the same amount of time on each section. For both the period study and the British depth study, it is important to have a time plan and to stick to it.

Look at the plan below. You could use this plan or develop your own and check it with your teacher. We have broken down the depth study into two 25 minute blocks of time. This is because some students spend too long on Questions 4(a) and 4(b). They then rush Question 4(c). However, the final question is worth the same amount of marks as 4(a) and 4(b) put together.

Section A (period study) Questions 1, 2 and 3: approx. 50 minutes

Section B (Option B1: Anglo-Saxon and Norman England, c1060–88) Question 4: approx. 50 minutes

Questions 4(a) and 4 (b): approx. 25 minutes

EITHER Question 4(c)(i) OR 4(c)(ii): approx. 25 minutes

Checking answers: 5 minutes

2 SPEND TIME DE-CODING QUESTIONS

The marks for each question are shown in brackets. This gives you an idea of how much you need to write, as does the space for your answer on the exam paper. However, do not panic if you do not fill all the space. There will probably be more space than you need and the quality of your answer is more important than how much you write. The most important thing is to keep focused on the question. If you include information that is not relevant to the question, you will not gain any marks, no matter how much you write!

Read each question carefully before you to start to answer it. Use the advice on de-coding questions on page 116 to make sure you focus on the question.

3 FOLLOW INSTRUCTIONS CAREFULLY

Read the instructions very carefully. Some students miss questions they need to answer, while others waste time answering more questions than they need to. Remember to answer Question 4(a) **AND** 4(b). You then need to choose between **EITHER** Question 4(c)(i) **OR** 4(c)(ii).

4 THE 'DESCRIBE' QUESTION

The first question on Section B asks you to describe two features of an aspect of the period you have studied. Headings on the exam paper help you to write about each feature separately. Advice on how to gain high marks on this type of question is on page 117.

5 THE 'EXPLAIN' QUESTION

The second question tests your ability to write effective explanations. You may be asked to explain why an event or development took place. Page 118 helps you to write a good answer to this type of question.

6 USING THE STIMULUS MATERIAL

When you attempt Question 4(b) and either Question 4(c)(i) or (c)(ii), you will have bullet points as stimulus material to help plan your answer. You do not have to include them, but try to use them to get you thinking and to support your arguments. You must bring in your own knowledge too. If you only use the stimulus material, you will not gain high marks for your answer.

7 THINK CAREFULLY ABOUT WHICH QUESTION YOU CHOOSE

When it comes to the choice of final question, do not rush your decision. Think carefully about which question you will do best on. Plan your answer – it is worth 16 marks, half the available marks for Section B of the exam paper.

8 THE 'JUDGEMENT' QUESTION

This question carries the most marks and requires a longer answer that needs careful planning. You will be provided with a statement and you will have to reach a judgement as to how far you agree with that statement. Pages 120–122 provide advice on answering this style of question.

CHECKING THE QUALITY OF YOUR WRITING

Make sure you leave five minutes at the end of the exam to check your answers. If you are short of time, check your answer to the final question first, as it carries the most marks. Page 123 provides advice on what to focus on. Remember that the accuracy of your spelling, punctuation and grammar is important in all questions, as it affects the clarity of your answer.

De-coding exam questions

The examiners are not trying to catch you out: they are giving you a chance to show what you know – and what you can do with what you know. However, you must stick to the question on the exam paper. Staying focused on the question is crucial. Including information that is not relevant, or misreading a question and writing about the wrong topic wastes time and gains you no marks.

To stay focused on the question, you will need to practise how to 'de-code' questions. This is particularly important for Section B of the exam paper. Follow these **five steps to success**:

Step 1 Read the question a couple of times. Then look at **how many marks** the question is worth. This tells you how much you are expected to write. Do not spend too long on questions only worth a few marks. Remember, it is worth planning the 12 and 16 mark questions.

Step 2 Identify the **conceptual** focus of the question. What is the key concept that the question focuses on? Is it asking you to look at:

- the **significance** of a discovery or individual
- **causation** – the reasons why an event or development happened
- **consequence** – the results of an event or development
- **similarities and differences** – between the key features of different periods
- **change** – the extent of change or continuity, progress or stagnation during a period?

Step 3 Spot the **question type**. Are you being asked to:

- **describe** – the key features of a period
- **explain** – similarities between periods or why something happened
- **reach a judgement** – as to how far you agree with a particular statement?

Each question type requires a different approach. Look for key words or phrases that help you to work out which approach is needed. The phrase 'How far do you agree?' means you need to weigh the evidence for and against a statement before reaching a balanced judgement. 'Explain why' means that you need to explore a range of reasons why an event happened.

Step 4 Identify the **content focus**. What is the area of content or topic the examiner wants you to focus on?

Step 5 Look carefully at the **date boundaries** of the question. What time period should you cover in your answer? Stick to this carefully or you will waste time writing about events that are not relevant to the question.

Look at the exam question below.

At first glance, it could appear that this question is only about William's use of violent methods to punish and keep control. This shows the danger of not de-coding a question carefully. If you simply describe examples of William's violent punishments, you will be missing the main focus of the question. If you explain why ferocity helped him to keep control, you would gain a few more marks, but you are still not focusing on the actual question.

The conceptual focus is causation – you need to reach a judgement on whether William's ferocious punishments were the main cause of William's control over England.

The content focus is more than just on William's ferocious methods. It is exploring a wider theme – the reasons for William's control over England 1066–75.

> **4(c)(i)** 'The main reason William I was able to keep control of England in the years 1066–75 was because of his ferocious punishment of rebels.' How far do you agree? Explain your answer. **(16)**

There are 16 marks available – this means the question requires an extended answer. It is definitely worth planning your answer to this question!

The dates provided for thinking about William's control are important. If you only think about causes of control in some of these years you will not be drawing your evidence from the whole era, which will cost you marks. The reasons why William was able to keep control differ depending on date and place, so a narrow focus won't show off your understanding.

The phrase 'How far do you agree' means that this question requires you to reach a judgement about the statement in quotation marks. This means analysing the impact of William's ferocious methods between 1066–75. It also means weighing the importance of this cause of control against other important causes (such as rival claimants to the throne being weak and lacking support, the appointment of Lanfranc).

REMEMBER

It is worth spending time de-coding questions carefully in the exam. It helps you focus on the question and stops you wasting time including information that is not relevant.

Further practice

Look at the other questions in Section B of the exam paper on page 114.

Break each question down into the five steps and check you have de-coded the question effectively.

Describing key features of a period

'Describe' questions only carry 4 marks, so it is important to get to the point quickly, so you do not waste precious time needed for questions that carry 12 or 16 marks.

> Look at the question below.
>
> Describe **two** features of Anglo-Saxon society. (4 marks)
> - Feature 1: _____
> - Feature 2: _____

Tip 1: stay relevant to the question

One major problem with 'Describe' questions is that students write too much! They include details that are not relevant to the question. Make sure you stick to the question – describing two key features of Anglo-Saxon society.

You do not need to:
- include more than two features (extra features will not gain you any more marks)
- evaluate and reach a judgement
- go beyond any date boundaries, if any are given

If you write too much, you could run out of time later in the exam when you are answering questions that are worth a lot more marks and need longer answers.

Tip 2: keep it short and simple

You can get two marks by simply identifying two features of Anglo-Saxon society.

For each feature you identify, add a sentence that adds further detail and develops your answer.

Look at the example below. Then practise your technique by tackling the examples in the exam practice box.

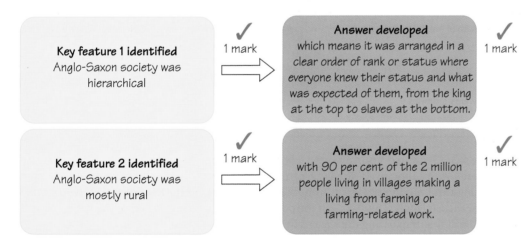

Key feature 1 identified
Anglo-Saxon society was hierarchical

✓ 1 mark

Answer developed
which means it was arranged in a clear order of rank or status where everyone knew their status and what was expected of them, from the king at the top to slaves at the bottom.

✓ 1 mark

Key feature 2 identified
Anglo-Saxon society was mostly rural

✓ 1 mark

Answer developed
with 90 per cent of the 2 million people living in villages making a living from farming or farming-related work.

✓ 1 mark

> ## Practice questions
>
> 1 Describe two features of Anglo-Saxon law and order.
> 2 Describe two features of William's army at the Battle of Hastings.
> 3 Describe two features of motte and bailey castles.
> 4 Describe two features of the Revolt of the Earls in 1075.
> 5 Describe two features of the feudal system.

REMEMBER

Stay focused and keep it short and simple. Four sentences are enough for four marks.

Writing effective explanations: tackling 12-mark 'Explain' questions

Look at the question below.

> **4(b)** Explain why there was a disputed succession to the English throne when Edward the Confessor died. (12 marks)
>
> You may use the following in your answer:
> * the wealth of Anglo-Saxon England
> * Harold Godwinson.
>
> You **must** also use information of your own.

The conceptual focus is on causation (explaining **why** something happened). The question is worth 12 marks. The examiner will expect you to give a range of reasons **why** there was a disputed succession to the English throne when Edward died.

It is important to spend time planning this question during your exam. Follow the steps below to help you plan effectively and produce a good answer.

Step 1: Get focused on the question

Make sure you de-code the question carefully. Note that the content focus is on the disputed succession crisis and the date boundary is 'when Edward the Confessor died' (i.e. January 1066). This means it will be necessary to consider events leading up to this date and shortly after. But don't write about Edward's reign as king, unless it directly relates to the crisis. Even if the question doesn't have an actual date written in it, there might be a sense of the date boundary – but you will need to activate your knowledge and work out the date period, just like in this question.

Step 2: Identify a range of factors

Try to cover more than one cause. If your mind goes blank, the stimulus bullet points can help you. For example, in the question above, 'the wealth of Anglo-Saxon England' should make you remember to explain how the country was rich from trade in precious metals, people were skilled in making jewellery and gold, and there were abundant farmlands and rivers for fish. Remember – you are expected to go beyond the bullet points and bring in your own knowledge – so do not be put off if a factor that you want to write about is not covered by the bullet points provided.

Step 3: Organise your answer using paragraphs

Do not worry about writing a long introduction. One or two sentences are more than enough and you can use words from the question. Look at the example below. Note how the student has built a short introduction into the first paragraph which focuses on quickly summarising the reasons for the succession crisis when Edward died.

> There was a disputed succession to the English throne when Edward died because not only did he die without a blood relative as a clear adult heir, we also cannot be certain that he named only one successor, possibly making promises to Harold Godwinson and William, Duke of Normandy. There were also other claimants, including Harald of Norway. With the wealth of Anglo-Saxon England as the prize, claimants were willing to challenge one another, turning 1066 into the year of succession crisis.

Aim to start a new paragraph each time you move on to a new factor that caused the defeat. Signpost your argument at the start of the paragraph. For example, you could start your next paragraph like this:

> In many ways Edward was himself to blame for the succession crisis that followed his death.

Step 4: Do not SAY that a factor was important – PROVE it was

Remember that a list of reasons for the succession crisis after Edward's death will not get you a high-level mark. You need to PROVE your case for each factor. This means developing your explanation by adding supporting information and specific examples (killer evidence).

This is where your work on connectives will come in useful. Look again at the advice on pages 32 and 123, and remember to tie what you know to the question by using connectives such as 'this meant that ...', 'this led to ...' and 'this resulted in ...'. For example, you may want to build on the opening to your first paragraph by proving what Edward did in his lifetime that made a crisis likely after his death.

> Edward did not have a son during his lifetime. Dying without a son might not have caused a crisis had Edward publically named a successor. In the 1050s Edward might have thought about identifying his great nephew Edgar Aethling as his successor, but this did not happen as Edgar was still a boy and lacked supporters or strong military experience to protect England. To complicate matters, Edward allegedly promised the throne to William in 1051, which he may also have repeated in 1064. But other sources suggest that when he was on his death bed Edward entrusted the kingdom to Harold. Therefore Edward's actions contributed to the succession crisis because there was a lack of certainty over who had the most right to be king which meant that rival claimants felt they had the right to challenge for the throne.

Step 5: End your answer with a thoughtful conclusion

Keep your conclusion short. A good conclusion makes the overall argument clear – it is not a detailed summary of everything you have already written! Make it clear which factor played the most important role. You may want to show how it links to other factors.

Advice	Model
Start by showing that you are aware that a range of factors played a role.	There was more than one reason for the succession crisis when Edward died. The wealth of Anglo-Saxon England attracted those who believed they had a claim and the fact that Harold quickly claimed the throne provoked others who thought they had a better claim.
Make it clear which factor you think played the most important role.	Ultimately, it was Edward's own actions that caused the crisis. Not producing an heir or publically naming an heir meant there was a gap, which claimants then battled to fill.
Support your argument with your key reason why you have come to this conclusion.	Had Edward publically named an heir, the dispute between Harold and William about who was to be king would have been settled. Naming an heir would also have removed the threats from claimants, like Harald of Norway, as there would be no vacant throne to claim.

Practice questions

You can find further practice questions on pages 46, 64, 75 and 107.

REMEMBER

Do not try to cover too many reasons for an event. Select which causes you can make the strongest argument for. Remember in the exam you would have approximately 15 minutes to answer this question.

Making judgements – tackling the 16-mark question

The last question on the exam paper carries the most marks and requires a carefully planned, detailed answer. You will be provided with a statement in quotation marks and asked to reach a judgement about **how far you agree** with it. The phrase 'how far' is important, as it is unlikely that you will totally agree or disagree with the statement. The examiner will be looking for you to show that you can weigh the evidence for and against the statement.

Look at the example below.

> **(c)(i)** 'The main consequence of the appointment of Lanfranc as Archbishop of Canterbury in 1070 was an increase in cathedral building.' How far do you agree? Explain your answer. (16 marks)
>
> You may use the following in your answer:
> - Archbishop Stigand
> - monasteries.
>
> You **must** also use information of your own.

Follow the same steps that you would for an 'explain' question (see page 118).

Step 1: focus

The content focus is important – you have to reach a judgement on the main consequences of Lanfranc's appointment as Archbishop of Canterbury. The conceptual focus is on consequences, so think broadly. You could think about social, economic, political and cultural consequences. Or maybe you could think about consequences for Norman control of England and consequences for the Church in England.

Step 2: Identify

The 16-mark questions require you to reach a judgement on a statement. In order to do this effectively, you need to identify **clear criteria** for reaching that judgement. Just like you need to cover a range of factors in 'explain' questions, you need to cover a **range of criteria** in 'judgement' questions.

Possible criteria for reaching a judgement:

- You could evaluate how wide-ranging the consequences were. Did the event have mainly religious consequences or were there important political, social or economic consequences as well?
- You could also analyse how many people were affected by the event. Did the changes affect all people in Norman England, or just those within the Church? Did Lanfranc provoke support or opposition?

Step 3: Organise

The simplest way to plan for judgement-style questions is to think in terms of 'for' and 'against' paragraphs:

Paragraph 1 – Evidence to **support** the statement. For example, show how the appointment of Lanfranc as Archbishop of Canterbury in 1070 did lead to an increase in cathedral building.

Paragraph 2 – Evidence to **counter** the statement. Show how Lanfranc's appointment generated many other consequences, far beyond cathedral buildings.

Paragraph 3 – Your final conclusion – weigh the evidence. How far do you agree with the statement?

Step 4: Prove

Remember to tie what you know to the question. Do not include information and think that it will speak for itself. Some students think that simply dropping in examples to the right paragraphs is enough. The following statement from a student could be further developed and gain more marks.

> Another important consequence of Lanfranc's appointment was the reforms of the Church that he implemented.

This does not **prove** that Lanfranc's appointment had important consequences. The student needs to go on to explain **how** the reforms of the Church affected people's lives in Norman England. The best way to do this would be to give precise examples of the reforms and to explain the impact of each one, specifying which people were affected and how. In other words, linking examples back to the theme of the consequences of Lanfranc's appointment.

Step 5: Conclude

Your conclusion is a crucial part of your answer. You have been asked to reach a judgement on a statement. You need to state clearly how far you agree with it and your reasons why. It would be easy to sit on the fence and avoid reaching a final conclusion. But sitting on the fence is a dangerous position. Your answer collapses and you lose marks.

Instead of sitting on the fence, you need to be confident and reach an overall judgement. Imagine that you have placed the evidence on a set of scales. How far do they tip in favour of the statement or against it?

You can then move on in your conclusion to explain your judgement. Do not repeat everything you have already written. Think of the scales – what are the heaviest pieces of evidence on each side? Build these into your conclusion in the following way:

Advice	Model
JUDGEMENT – Start with your judgement – try to incorporate words from the question into this sentence.	I disagree that the main consequence of Lanfranc's appointment as Archbishop was an increase in cathedral building.
COUNTER – Show that you are aware that there is some evidence to counter this and give the best example.	Some people might argue that cathedral building was the main consequence because it was the most visible, physical impact on England that Lanfranc achieved.
SUPPORT – Explain why, overall, you have reached the judgement you have. Give your key reason or reasons why.	But, just because cathedral building was the most visible sign of Lanfranc's work does not make it the main consequence of Lanfranc's appointment. He led the Normalisation of the English Church, stamped out corruption, and kept the Pope's influence at bay to ensure William was as powerful as possible in England. He also helped William secure his power by being instrumental in defeating the Revolt of the Earls in 1075. Overall, he helped William to conquer England.

Practice questions

You can find further practice questions on pages 46, 64, 75 and 107.

REMEMBER

Two important warnings:

Firstly, leave enough time to **check your answer** carefully for spelling, punctuation and grammar.

- Is your spelling and punctuation accurate?
- Does your work make sense? Are your arguments clear?
- Have you used a wide range of historical terms?

Secondly, **beware of iceberg questions!**

Spot the part of the question that lurks beneath the water. Remember what we said about de-coding 'judgement' questions like the one here:

(c)(i) 'The main reason William I was able to keep control of England in the years 1066–75 was because of his ferocious punishment of rebels'. How far do you agree? Explain your answer.   (16 marks)

Remember what we said about de-coding 'judgement' questions like the one above? You need to identify the causes lurking beneath the surface, then weigh the importance of the cause in the question (the one on the surface) against the importance of other causes such as the weaknesses of revolts against him, how the Normans won the support of the Anglo-Saxons, and the use of motte and bailey castles.

123

What are the key ingredients of effective writing in GCSE history?

The language you use to express your ideas is very important. One of the ways to get better at History is to be more precise with your use of language. For example, rather than simply saying that you **agree** or **disagree** with a statement, you can use language that shows whether you agree to **a large extent** or only to **some extent**. Look at the different shades of argument below and experiment with using some of the phrases. Use them when you are debating or discussing in class.

Strong language

Tentative language

Thinking carefully about the language you use

Varying your language to show how far you agree with a statement:
I totally/entirely/completely/absolutely agree with …
I substantially/fundamentally/strongly agree with …
I agree to a large extent with … I mainly/mostly agree with …
I agree to some extent with … I partially/partly agree with …
I only agree with … to a limited/slight extent.

Varying your language to show how important a factor/cause is:
… was by far the most important reason why …
The key/crucial/essential factor was …
… was the main cause of … The most influential cause was …
… played a significant/important/major role in …
… was of some importance in …

Varying your language to show the significance or importance of an individual, discovery, event or development:
… made the most important/significant contribution to …
… had a crucial/major/highly significant impact on …
… had an important/influential impact on …
… was of some importance/significance
… only made a limited/partial/slight/minimal contribution to …

Varying your language to show the extent of change:
… was revolutionised in … / … totally changed during …
… was transformed during … / ,… there was fundamental change in …
The period saw significant/important progress in …
… saw some changes/progress in …
… saw limited/slight/minimal progress in …

Helpful phrases and sentence starters		
When you want to explore the other side of an argument:	**When you want to highlight similarities:**	**When you want to make an additional point to support an argument:**
On the other hand …	In the same way …	Also … Additionally …
However …	Similarly …	In addition …
Alternatively, it could be argued that …	This is similar to the way that …	Moreover …
	Likewise …	Furthermore …
When you want to link points or show that one thing led to another:	**When you want to give examples to support a point:**	**When you want to show that an individual, event or discovery was important:**
Therefore … Due to …	For example … For instance …	… was a crucial turning point in …
Consequently … One consequence of this was …	This can be seen when …	… acted as an important catalyst for …
This caused … This led to … This resulted in … This meant that …	This is clearly shown by …	Without this event/development/discovery … would not have happened.
	This is supported by … This is proven by …	This had an immediate impact on …
		In the short term, this transformed/revolutionised …
		In the long term, this had a lasting impact on …

Self-assessing and peer-assessing your work

It is important that you check your own work before you hand it to your teacher to be marked. Sometimes you may be asked to assess the work of someone else in your class. In both cases, you need to know what you are looking for.

What are the key ingredients of great writing in history? You can use the **bingo card** as a checklist – get competitive and try to show that you have covered all the squares and got a full house of ingredients!

The answer starts with a **clear focus on the question** (there is no long introduction). Key words from the question are used during the answer. For longer answers, each paragraph is linked to the question.	Statements and arguments are fully developed and explained – showing good knowledge and understanding. Arguments are **well supported** by accurate, relevant and well-selected evidence.	**Connectives** are used to help prove arguments and show significance/impact. Look for phrases like: *this led to …* *this resulted in …* *this meant that …*
There is a **clear line of argument** at the start of each paragraph – think of it as a signpost for what follows. The rest of the paragraph supports this argument. The line of argument flows throughout the answer, building up to a clear conclusion.	Paragraphs have been used to provide a **clear structure**. Each paragraph starts with • a different cause/factor (12-mark 'explain' questions) or • a different theme/criteria (16-mark 'judgement' questions).	The answers shows **wide-ranging** knowledge and understanding. It considers a range of factors/causes ('explain' questions) or explores the evidence for **and** against a statement ('judgement' questions).
The language used helps to construct very precise arguments – showing how important the writer thinks a cause/factor, event or individual is. A good range of specialist **historical vocabulary** has been used.	There is a **clear conclusion**. For 'explain' questions, factors/causes are prioritised or linked. For 'judgement' questions, there is a focus on 'how far' the writer agrees with the statement.	The answer has been **carefully checked** for spelling, punctuation and grammar. The meaning is always clear throughout the answer.

You can use the **progression grid** below to get an idea of what getting better at history looks like. This is designed to give you a general idea of what you need to do to produce good answers in the exam. It focuses on the four key things in the white squares on the bingo card.

The history progression grid

	Question focus	Organisation	Line of argument	Supporting information
High level	The answer is consistently focused on the question.	The answer is structured very carefully and explanations are coherent throughout the answer.	The line of argument is very clear and convincing. It flows throughout the answer.	Supporting information has been precisely selected and shows wide-ranging knowledge and understanding.
	The answer is mainly focused on the question.	The answer is well organised, but some parts of the answer lack coherence.	The line of argument is clear, convincing and generally maintained through the answer.	Supporting information is accurate and relevant, and shows good knowledge and understanding.
	The answer has weak or limited links to the question.	Some statements are developed and there is some attempt to organise the material.	The line of argument is partly convincing, but not maintained through the answer.	Supporting information is mainly accurate and relevant, and shows some knowledge and understanding.
	The answer has no real links to the question.	The answer lacks organisation.	The line of argument is unclear or missing.	Supporting information is limited or not relevant.

Glossary

Abbey   The buildings where monks or nuns lived and prayed.

Anglo-Saxon   Name given to the period and people in England before the Norman Conquest.

Ambassador   A person sent to discuss important matters with the ruler of another country.

Anoint   To sprinkle with holy oil during a ceremony such as a coronation.

Bayeux Tapestry   An embroidery telling the story of the Norman Conquest (see page 8).

Beacon fire   A large fire lit to send warnings quickly over long distances.

Bishopric   An area under the control of a bishop, one of the leading men in the Church.

Blasphemy   Words that insult or show contempt for God, including swear-words.

Breton   Anyone from Brittany, a region in northern France.

Cavalry   Soldiers who fight on horseback.

Chaplain   A priest who holds services for a king or nobleman and his family.

Chronicler   Usually a monk who wrote an account of events he thought were important to remember.

Civil war   A war between two groups of people in one country.

Coronation   The ceremony when a king or queen is crowned at the beginning of a reign.

Crusade   The wars fought by Christian soldiers to gain control of Jerusalem.

Demesne   The land owned by a king or lord that he kept to grow his own food and keep animals on.

Domesday Book   Manuscript that records the results of the Domesday Survey (see page 92).

Domesday Survey   The process of collecting the information summarised in the Domesday Book.

Duchy   The area governed by a duke, a powerful ruler in France.

Earl   The most powerful noblemen in England in the eleventh century.

Embassy   A group of people sent to discuss important matters with a foreign ruler.

Export   Sell or exchange abroad.

Fief   An area of land held by an individual from his lord or king.

Forfeiture   Being forced to hand over land and castles to the king.

Garrison   Soldiers who lived in and defended a castle.

Genocide   The deliberate killing of very large groups of people, especially those of one nationality or religion.

Holy Days   Religious festivals such as Christmas, Easter or saints' Days when people did not work.

'Hue and cry'   The process of chasing someone thought to have committed a crime (see page 15).

Import   To buy goods such as wine or cloth from foreign countries and bring it to England.

Infantry   Soldiers who fought on foot.

Jester   An entertainer.

Knight service   The amount of time a knight or soldier was on duty for his lord each year. In return he received land from his lord (see page 81).

Labour service   The farming work done by villagers for their lord. In return they received lands on which they grew food for themselves.

Mercenary   A soldier who fought for wages rather than because he owed knight service to his lord.

Minstrel   A singer or musician.

Motte and bailey castle   An early type of castle built after 1066 (see page 55).

Nobles   The richest and most powerful landowners in the country.

Papal banner   A flag given by the Pope to show he supported an individual such as William of Normandy.

Patron saint   A saint associated with a particular place, church or group of people.

Pilgrimage   A journey to a holy place to pray and perhaps ask God for forgiveness.

Pillage   To raid and steal, often with violence.

Plunder   To raid and steal, often with violence.

Reeve   An Anglo-Saxon official in a county (shire-reeve) or village.

Regent   The deputy for a king while he was abroad.

Relic   Part of the body of a saint or other holy person or an object belonging to a saint.

Saint   A person whom the Church has said lived a life of great holiness.

Saints' days   Days dedicated to celebrating the lives of individual saints e.g. St. Andrew's Day.

Shield wall   A defensive tactic in battle when soldiers interlinked shields to form a wall and blunt attacks.

Tanner   Someone who makes leather or leather goods.

Treason   Planning to kill or harm the king or one of his family.

Whit   A religious festival held on the seventh Sunday after Easter.

Witan   Powerful lords and bishops who were the advisers of Anglo-Saxon kings.

Index